Air Fryer Cookbook for Beginners #2019

Easy, Healthy, and Low Carb Air Fryer Recipes That Are Easy-To-Remember – Made for Very Busy People

Disclaimer

You've downloaded this book because you want to get your hands on some awesome recipes which will keep you nourished and taste amazing *without* leaving you chained to the stove.

But you also want to enjoy recipes you can create with your air fryer which are also low carb and will help you stay in shape, keep you healthy and boost your performance in all areas of your life. You don't want much, do you?? Just kidding.

That's why I've written this straightforward, easy-to-understand air fryer cookbook for beginners.

Because I know you want all this stuff and I know you absolutely deserve it.

You work hard. You play hard. Your diet needs to do the same, right?

So, I'll whizz though this boring bit as quickly as possible. Just remember that, despite all my expertise and skill in the kitchen, I'm not a medical professional and I'm not qualified to give you medical advice. For that reason, please consult a medical professional before taking part in this diet, especially if you have a pre-existing health problem. By following this diet, you agree to do so at your own risk and assume all associated risk involved.

The information in this book is for informational purposes only and is not intended to be construed as medical advice nor should it replace the guidance of a qualified instructor who can guide you personally and tailor a low carb diet program to your specific requirements. Bear in mind that there are no 'typical' results from the information provided - as individuals differ, the results will differ.

No responsibility is taken for any loss or damage related directly or indirectly to the information in this book. Never disregard professional medical advice or delay in seeking it because of something you have read in this book or in any linked materials.

Copyright © 2019 xxx

All rights reserved. No part of this publication may be reproduced, distributed, or transmitted in any form or by any means, including photocopying, recording, or other electronic or mechanical methods, without the prior written permission of the publisher.

Table of Contents

INTRODUCTION 6
Overwhelm 6
The crash 7
My life changed 7
Why I wrote this book 8
LOW CARB AIR FRYING- WHAT YOU NEED TO KNOW 9
What's an Air Fryer? 9
How do you use an air fryer? 9
What is the low carb diet? 10
How to do the low carb diet 10
RECIPES 12
Breakfasts 12
    Breakfast Pizza 12
    Chili Cream Soufflé 13
    Vegan French "Toast" 14
    Sweet Potato Hash 15
    Toad-in-the-Hole Tarts 16
    Tex-Mex Hash Browns 17
    Cheese and Bacon Breakfast Bombs 18
    Vegan Breakfast Sandwich 19
    Soft- & Hard-Boiled Eggs 20
    Cajun Breakfast Sausage 21
    Cheese and Red Pepper Egg Cups 22
    Breakfast Stuffed Peppers 23
    Sausage Breakfast Casserole 24
Pork 25
    Pork Milanese 25
    Moroccan Style Pork Tenderloin 26
    Crispy Parmesan Crusted Pork Chops 27
    Cheesy Pork Chop Fries 28
    Pork Tonkatsu 29
    Memphis-Style BBQ Pork Ribs 30
    Chinese Salt and Pepper Pork Chops 31
    Rack of Lamb with Mint and Honey 32
    Honey Mustard Pork Chops 33
    Cajun Cheese Pork Chops 34
    Pork Belly 35
    Scotch Eggs 36
Beef 37
    Steak with Garlic Herb Butter 37
    Coffee & Spice Ribeye Steak 38
    Carne Asada 39

Beef Satay	40
Beef Bulgogi Burgers	41
Bourbon Bacon Burger	42
Beef Steak Kebabs	44
Rib Eye Steak with Blue Cheese Butter	45
Beef Lasagna	46
Keto Steak Nuggets	47
Chicken and Turkey	**48**
Baked Chicken Nuggets with Crunchy Almond Dip	48
BBQ Chicken Wings	49
Buffalo Chicken Legs	50
Chicken Coconut Meatballs	51
Jalapeno Popper Stuffed Chicken Breast	52
Bagel Chicken Roll-Ups	53
Tandoori Chicken	54
Spicy Mexican Chicken Burgers	55
Easy Piri-Piri Chicken	56
Adobo Air Fried Chicken Thighs	57
Spicy Popcorn Chicken	58
Italian Chicken Tenders	59
Easy Low Carb Turkey Meatballs	60
Sage and Rosemary Fried-Turkey Wings	61
Turkey Breast	62
Lamb	**63**
Simple Lamb Chops	63
Lamb and Spinach Meatballs with Tzatziki	64
Moroccan Lamb Burgers	66
Rosemary and Garlic Rack of Lamb	67
Mojito Lamb Kabobs	68
Lamb Kofta Kabab	69
Fish and Seafood	**70**
Tuna Patties	70
Thai Fish Cakes	71
Crispy Fish Sticks	72
Coconut Shrimp	73
Curried Salmon Cakes	74
Perfect Air Fryer Salmon	75
Cilantro Lime Air Fryer Shrimp	76
Parmesan Shrimp	77
Cajun Crispy Golden Fish	78
Vegetarian & Vegan	**79**
Lupini Falafal	79
Super Crispy Air Fryer Tofu	80
Vegan Mini Veggie Burritos	81

- Tofu Satay with Peanut Butter Sauce ... 82
- Ginger Tofu Sushi Bowl ... 83
- Asian Vegetable Spring Rolls ... 85
- Broccoli Tofu Scramble ... 87
- Crunchy Panko Tofu ... 88
- Thai Veggie Bites ... 89
- Portobello Mushroom Pizzas ... 91
- Thai-Style Vegan Crab Cakes ... 92
- Cauliflower Chickpea Tacos ... 93

Side Dishes ... 94
- Crispy Balsamic Brussels Sprouts ... 94
- Maple Syrup Bacon ... 95
- Fried Asparagus with Spicy Mayo Dip ... 96
- Feta Psiti Greek Baked Feta ... 97
- Avocado Fries ... 98
- Onion Rings ... 99
- Roasted Asian Broccoli ... 100
- Air Fryer Fried Pickles ... 101
- Bacon and Cream Cheese Stuffed Jalapeno Poppers ... 102
- Cauliflower Buffalo Wings ... 103
- Healthy French Fries ... 104
- Healthy Zucchini Corn Fritters ... 105
- Eggplant Parmesan ... 106
- Roasted Brussels Sprouts with Garlic and Thyme ... 107
- Special Cauliflower Rice ... 108
- Baked Sweet Potato Cauliflower Patties ... 109
- Tortilla Snack Chips ... 110
- Cheese Sticks ... 111

Sweets and Treats ... 112
- Easy Coconut Pie ... 112
- Cinnamon Donuts ... 113
- Gluten-Free Chocolate Lava Cake ... 114
- Fried Cheesecake Bites ... 115
- Chocolate Almond Cupcakes ... 116
- Brazilian Grilled Pineapple ... 117
- Spiced Apples ... 118
- Flourless Chocolate Brownies ... 119
- Sweet Potato Dessert Fries ... 120

FINAL WORDS ... 121

Introduction

We've all been there, haven't we?

You've had a hard day and all you want to do is collapse onto the sofa, eat whatever the hell you fancy and then collapse into bed for a well-deserved night's sleep. You don't want to be spending hours in the kitchen slaving away, just so you can eat healthy.

Your meals need to be super-simple, easy to make and almost effortless. They need to be quick to make. They need to be on the table fast. If they're inexpensive, that's even better. And healthy and nutritious is also a bit bonus too.

But at this point, you really don't care.

You've been running around all day, ticking those chores off your 'to do' list, keeping your boss or clients happy, taking care of your loved ones, trying to find time to work a high-pressure career, to crush those workouts, to stay productive *and* position yourself a the top of your game…

It's not easy to be a highly successful and fulfilled individual, is it?

As you and I both know, this kind of lifestyle is far from sustainable over the long-term. You'll only push yourself towards burnout, overwhelm and sickness if you carry on as you are.

You can't do everything and be everything. Something has usually got to give, and it's usually your healthy eating habits.

Even though you want to be healthy, you really do, you find yourself eating junk food or heading to grab takeout or heading to the drive-thru, just to keep some food in your body. You make poor food choices just because you don't have the time to waste.

But it doesn't have to be this way.

Invest in an air fryer, learn the art of air fryer cooking (by reading this book!) and you can stick to your healthy, low carb diet without needing to spend hours in the kitchen or forcing yourself to eat food that you hate just because it's quick.

I'm speaking from experience here.

Overwhelm

Not too long ago, I was up to my eyeballs in work and life commitments. So much so that I barely had time to cook.

I was that busy mom, juggling the responsibilities of bringing up two kids, working long hours in a career I'd worked so hard to get off the ground and struggling to hold it all together. I seemed to do OK, though.

Sure- my sleep suffered, I never spend enough time with my kids, and I used to daydream of sailing off into the sunset, just so I could get some private time for myself.

But I seemed to be managing to hold it all together. Just.

So what if each and every one of our meals was takeout? Did it matter that I was slowly piling on the pounds and starting to struggle to do up the top button on my jeans? Did it matter that my eczema was starting to flare up like never before? Not really. I just didn't care.

Until my world came crashing down around my ears.

The crash

It was a normal day for me. I'd just dropped my kids off at day care at a stupid-early time. I'd grabbed myself a huge coffee and I was battling through my rush-hour commute to work, huge multi-million-dollar projects looming over my head. Although my adrenaline levels were sky high, I barely noticed it anymore- I'd been running on empty for a long time and I'd learned to brush off the feelings over overwhelm.

Then it happened. The crash.

In a few seconds, my life flashed before me and I found myself sat in shock in a car smoking profusely from the bonnet, with a smashed up rear windshield behind me and a ton of chaos happening outside.

Luckily, the accident wasn't my fault and I wasn't injured. But still, I couldn't move.

It was as if someone had hit pause and I couldn't continue. All the stress and overwhelm in my life had finally caught up with me and I was broken. Beaten. I knew I couldn't go on as I had.

My life changed

So, I sat back and reassessed my life. I figured out what needed to change to help me feel like my old self again, free from the madness. I cut down on my hours at work, I started getting more exercise, I prioritized time with my kids, and I started to eat more healthily.

Even though my life became calmer, I still didn't want to spend hours in the kitchen.

I knew that there had to be a way to slash the amount of time and effort it took to create delicious and nutritious food. It was just a case of finding it.

The answer came in the unlikely form of an air fryer. I was given one as a birthday gift, and as soon as I unwrapped it, I know that this was the answer I had been looking for!

I could cook healthy food and it didn't need to take long at all! I could nourish myself, lose weight, feel great and still do everything else I wanted to, without sacrificing a thing. It sounds like a bit of a cliché to say it, but the air fryer really did change my life.

Why I wrote this book

I know that I'm not the only person to have struggled with balancing the demands of life with wanting to eat a healthy diet (and usually failing).

So, I decided to write this book! I'm here to share with you all the mouth-watering, delicious, and at times, utterly indulgent recipes that you can make in your air fryer quickly and easily. It will make your life a million times easier, help you shift weight and give you that push you need to take better care of yourself.

At the beginning of this book I've included some general information about air fryers and also the low carb diet so you can get started quickly and easily.

Then I'll get right onto the recipes themselves and share with you a ton of versatile, fast and delicious meals you can make with nothing more than your air fryer and a handful of delicious ingredients.

I'll include everything from breakfasts, to chicken, lamb, beef, pork and seafood dishes, and include plenty of options to keep vegetarians and vegan happy too. I've also included some yummy desert and treat recipes at the end to keep you feeling utterly spoiled.

Enjoy yourself and get cooking!

Low Carb Air Frying- What You Need to Know

Before we jump into the recipes, I'd like to first share with you some background information so that you can start using your air fryer with ease straight away. Whilst using one is by no means complicated, it always helps to get an overview before you get stuck in, including exactly what an air fryer is and how you can use it.

But I'm not just going to be talking about the air fryers here. I'll also give you a very brief introduction into the low carb diet and how it can help you to stay healthy, lose weight, get your energy levels back on high and look and feel at your best.

Shall we get started?

What's an Air Fryer?

If you're reading this book, it's highly likely that you already know what an air fryer is. After all, that's what made you pick up this book in the first place, right?

But to explain to those of you who don't know, an air fryer is just like a deep fat fryer, but instead of heating oil to high temperatures to cook your food, it heats air.

The result is deep fried food with just a fraction of the calories, none of the unhealthy fats. You'll still enjoy the same amazingly crunchy texture and beautiful flavors that you know and love without worrying so much about your waistline or your heart.

The air fryer is the perfect addition to a minimalist, conscious kitchen and it's also very versatile machine, allowing you roast, bake and grill your favorite foods with ease (yes, even chocolate lava cake!). Your only limitation is your imagination!

They are rather large kitchen appliances though, so make sure you have enough space before you head out there and buy one. They generally cost between $100-300, depending on the model, although you might be able to find one second-hand somewhere like Craigslist or eBay.

How do you use an air fryer?

Don't worry- there's absolutely no learning curve when it comes to using your air fryer. Simply plug it in, set the temperature, prepare your food, place the food into the basket, and let it work its magic for the required time. Then simply serve and enjoy. That's it!

Whilst you don't need to use any oil, you can spray a small amount directly into the machine for a touch of added crunch or taste. There are a few places within the recipes where I'll suggest that you do this for best results, but feel free to leave it out if you'd prefer or to add a quick spray if that's what you'd prefer.

Remember, this is your food, your life. Whilst I can help nudge you in the direction of inspiration and health, it's up to you to make it happen and work best for you!

What is the low carb diet?

Now let's talk for a few moments about the low carb diet.

Despite what the name might suggest, the low carb diet is actually much more than a weight-loss diet. It's a lifestyle.

Because unlike many other diets, it doesn't demand that you ditch all your favorite foods or start living off carrot stick and lettuce. No one is going to tell you to ditch all your favorite foods because you can carry right on eating them!

A more relaxed and low-key version of popular diets such as the Ketogenic Diet, the Atkins Diet or LCHF, it asks you to reduce your carb count as much as you can without getting super strict or restrictive about it.

This means you can still enjoy many of the weight loss and health benefits that other low-carbers boast AND you can still include medium-carb foods like potatoes, carrots and fruits if you want to. You'll include healthy amounts of brain-friendly fats to keep you looking and feeling at your best.

The secret is to keep it all balanced, including a wide variety of nourishing and delicious foods and you will lose weight, boost your energy, clear up any chronic health issues, improve your sleep, get stronger, improve your endurance and athletic performance and even rebalance your hormones, clear up your skin and if you're a women, banish PMS too.

Low carb is brilliant.

How to do the low carb diet

It's really easy to follow this diet. Simply...

Reduce or avoid sugar, overly sweet fruits and high carb vegetables, starchy foods like bread, pasta, rice, beans and potatoes, dried fruits, fruit juices and highly processed foods.

Enjoy plenty of meat, fish, eggs, tofu and vegetables which grow above the ground. Include plenty of natural fats like butter and avocados. Eat whenever you like, without counting calories or weighing your food. Cook from scratch as much as possible and eat until you're satisfied.

Remember, there are no restrictions when it comes to low carb- it's a much more relaxed diet than the Keto or Atkins diet. If you decide that you want to treat yourself to a few more carbs one meal, you go ahead and do it. Life is to be lived to the full!

Can everyone follow a low carb diet?
Yes, almost everyone can safely follow a low carb diet. However, if you're diabetic, suffer from high blood pressure, you're pregnant or breastfeeding, please do contact a medical professional before starting a low carb diet.

Hang on! The low carb diet is about eating more fat, yet the air fryer is all about using less fat...What's going on here?
I knew you'd ask that! The answer is, not all fats are made the same and they're not all bad. We actually need to them to help us produce the hormones necessary to keep our bodies working efficiently and to keep us looking and feeling great.

Instead of ditching them completely from our diets, we need to eat more of the healthy types of fats and less of those unhealthy fats if we want to achieve optimal health.

The good news is that those healthy fats are very easy to identify. They're the type of fats which haven't been overly processed or tampered with and so remain very close to their natural state. This includes food such as avocados, butter, cheese, oily fish, coconut oil, eggs, and nuts and seeds. These foods are high in omega 3 fatty acids which help build your brain and your nervous system, they provide healthy energy and they also provide your body with many other fat-based nutrients such as vitamin E.

However, we do need to start reducing our intake of those unhealthy fats. These are the ones that are highly processed or altered and look nothing like their original form. This category includes those highly processed vegetable oils and margarines, processed food products like biscuits, potato chips and pies which can become carcinogenic when heated to high temperatures.

Using an air fryer will allow you to increase your consumption of those healthy fats whilst decreasing your consumption of the unhealthy fats yet still enjoy delicious foods. As I'm sure you'll agree, this is a revelation when it comes to achieving optimal health! It's exciting stuff!

Now we've quickly run through everything you need to get started, let's not hang around here talking. Let's dive right into the recipes and start feeling inspired!

RECIPES

Breakfasts

Breakfast Pizza

If you're following the Keto diet, you want to keep your carbs super-low, but you want to have an epic breakfast, check out the following. It's perfect for meat-lovers and will keep you satisfied for hours.

Serves: 4
Time: 20 mins
- Calories: 320
- Net carbs: 2g
- Protein: 40g
- Fat: 45g

Ingredients:
- 2 oz. cream cheese
- 2 cups mozzarella, shredded
- 2 free-range eggs, beaten
- 1 cup almond flour
- Pinch salt & pepper
- 6 strips cooked bacon
- 4 sausage links, cooked and diced
- 2 deli ham slices, diced
- ½ cup mozzarella cheese
- ¼ cup shredded cheddar

Method:
1. Preheat your air fryer to 400°F and grease a springform pan that will fit into your air fryer.
2. Grab a medium bowl and add the cream cheese and mozzarella. Pop into the microwave for one minute and stir well until combined. Pop to one side.
3. Take a medium bowl and add the almond flour and the eggs. Stir to combine.
4. Add the cheese mixture and stir well.
5. Push into the springform pan and press down well.
6. Pop into the air fryer for 10 minutes and cook until set.
7. Remove from the fryer and add the remaining toppings.
8. Pop back into the air fryer and cook for a further 10-15 minutes until cooked.
9. Serve and enjoy!

Chili Cream Soufflé

Treat yourself to something truly special by creating this light, fluffy and satisfying breakfast soufflé. Perfect for cold winter mornings, it will wake up your taste buds and help you feel utterly spoiled. Enjoy!

Serves: 4
Time: 10 mins
- Calories: 127
- Net carbs: 3g
- Protein: 10g
- Fat: 7g

Ingredients:
- 4 free-range eggs
- 4 tablespoon cream
- Large pinch red chili pepper
- Fresh parsley, chopped
- Salt and pepper, to taste

Method:
1. Preheat your air fryer to 390 °F and grease some ramekin dishes.
2. Take a large bowl and add the eggs, whisking well to combine.
3. Add the cream, parsley and chili and stir well to combine.
4. Pour the egg mixture into the ramekin dishes up to about half way.
5. Pop into the air fryer and cook for 8-10 minutes until perfect.
6. Serve and enjoy.

Vegan French "Toast"

Could there ever be anything better than French toast for breakfast? We think not! Even if you're vegan or following a plant-based diet, you can still enjoy the cinnamon-sweetness to start the day without all those carbs!

Serves: 2
Time: 25 mins

- Calories: 258
- Net carbs: 5g
- Protein: 25g
- Fat: 13g

Ingredients:

- 1 block extra firm tofu
- ½ cup coconut flour
- ¼ cup granulated Monk Fruit sweetener
- 1 tablespoon cinnamon

Method:

1. Start by preheating your air fryer to 350°F.
2. Next remove the tofu from the packaging and squeeze to remove any excess liquid. Place to one side to drain.
3. Grab a medium bowl and add the coconut flour, sweetener and cinnamon. Stir well to mix.
4. Place the tofu onto a chopping board and cut in half, then half again, creating triangular pieces.
5. Pop each piece into the cinnamon sugar mixture and coat well then place into your air fryer.
6. Cook for 7 minutes, flipping halfway through to cook evenly.
7. Serve and enjoy!

Sweet Potato Hash

Sweet potatoes make a great filling breakfast that's packed with antioxidants and bursting with taste. Add bacon and some smoky paprika and you'll have a treat waiting for you!

Serves: 2-4
Time: 20 mins
- Calories: 131
- Net carbs: 12g
- Protein: 2g
- Fat: 9g

Ingredients:
- 2 large sweet potato, cut into small cubes
- 2 slices bacon, cut into small pieces
- 2 tablespoon olive oil
- 1 tablespoon smoked paprika
- 1 teaspoon sea salt
- 1 teaspoon ground black pepper
- 1 teaspoon dried dill weed

Method:
1. Preheat your air fryer to 400°F.
2. Grab a large bowl and combine all the ingredients, stirring well.
3. Pop into the air fryer and cook for 15 minutes, turning often until evenly cooked.
4. Serve and enjoy!

Toad-in-the-Hole Tarts

Yep, these easy air fryer tarts are pretty high calorie but they make up for it with buckets of nutrition and tons of flavor. Fragrant chives, mouth-watering cheese, nourishing ham and eggs...what more could you want for breakfast?

Serves: 4
Time: 30 mins
- Calories: 650
- Net carbs: 15g
- Protein: 12g
- Fat: 27g

Ingredients:
- 1 sheet frozen low carb puff pastry, thawed
- 4 tablespoon shredded Cheddar cheese
- 4 tablespoon diced cooked ham
- 4 free-range eggs
- Chopped fresh chives (opt)

Method:
1. Preheat your air fryer to 400°F.
2. Remove the pastry from the packaging and unfold. Cut into four equal pieces.
3. Place into your air fryer and cook for 5 minutes then remove and pop onto a plate.
4. Use the back of a spoon to carefully make a small dent in the pastry. Add 1 tablespoon each of cheese and ham, then cover with an egg.
5. Place back into the air fryer basket and cook again for 5 minutes until perfectly cooked.
6. Remove and leave to cool then serve and enjoy.

Tex-Mex Hash Browns

You really can't go wrong when you have hash browns for breakfast, especially when they're packed with Mexican spice and they're healthy too! Super-easy and utterly delicious, they'll give you a burst of vitamin C and healthy carbs that will keep you fueled through anything!

Serves: 4
Time: 30 mins
- Calories: 247
- Net carbs: 49g
- Protein: 6g
- Fat: 5g

Ingredients:
- 1 ½ lb. potatoes, peeled and cut into 1" cubes
- 1 tablespoon olive oil
- 1 red bell pepper, seeded and cut into 1" pieces
- 1 small onion, cut into 1" pieces
- 1 jalapeno, seeded and cut into 1" rings
- ½ teaspoon olive oil
- ½ teaspoon taco seasoning mix
- ½ teaspoon ground cumin
- 1 pinch salt and ground black pepper, to taste

Method:
1. Preheat your air fryer to 320°F.
2. Grab a large bowl and add the potatoes and 1 tablespoon of oil. Stir well.
3. Place into the air fryer and cook for 18 minutes.
4. Meanwhile, place the bell pepper, onion and jalapeno into a bowl and add ½ teaspoon of oil plus the cumin, salt, pepper and taco seasoning. Stir well to coat.
5. Remove the potatoes from the air fryer and place into the bowl with the peppers. Stir well.
6. Return all the veggies back to the air fryer and cook on 356°F for 6 minutes.
7. Serve and enjoy.

Cheese and Bacon Breakfast Bombs

There's just one word for these breakfast bombs- YUM! Everyone loves them, they look super-cute and they're lots of fun to make too. Enjoy!

Serves: 2
Time: 25 mins
- Calories: 305
- Net carbs: 23g
- Protein: 19g
- Fat: 15g

Ingredients:
- 3 center-cut bacon slices
- 3 large eggs, lightly beaten
- 1 oz. cream cheese, softened
- 1 tablespoon chopped fresh chives
- 4 oz. low carb pizza dough
- Cooking spray

Method:
1. Pop a pan over a medium heat and cook the bacon for ten minutes until crisp.
2. Remove from the heat and crumble, then pop to one side.
3. Add the eggs to the pan and stir often, cooking until set. Remove from the heat.
4. Place the eggs into a bowl with the cream cheese, chives and bacon.
5. Preheat your air fryer to 350°F.
6. Next take the pizza dough and carefully cut it into four pieces.
7. Roll each piece into a circle.
8. Place ¼ of the egg mixture into the middle and fold over the sides of the dough to meet in the middle.
9. Pop into the air fryer and cook for 5 minutes until perfectly cooked.

Vegan Breakfast Sandwich

Rich in plant-friendly nutrients and as much taste as you can handle, this breakfast sandwich is perfect piled up with as many ingredients as your heart desires. If you're looking to keep the carb count down, simply sub the muffins with a low carb bread substitute of your choice.

Serves: 4
Time: 20 mins

- Calories: 325
- Net carbs: 45g
- Fat: 10g
- Protein: 32g

Ingredients:

- 1 block extra firm tofu
- ¼ cup light soy sauce
- 1 teaspoon garlic powder
- ½ teaspoon turmeric
- Dash of paprika
- 4 low carb English muffins
- 1 Haas avocado, sliced

To serve...

- 4 slices vegan cheese
- Sliced onion
- Sliced tomato

Method:

1. Remove the tofu from the packet and squeeze to remove excess liquid. Leave for ten minutes to drain.
2. Slice the tofu into four pieces then pop to one side.
3. Find a shallow dish and add the soy sauce, garlic, turmeric and paprika. Stir well.
4. Place the tofu into the marinade and pop into the fridge for 10 minutes to marinate.
5. Preheat the air fryer to 400°F.
6. Remove the tofu from the marinade and allow any excess liquid to drain.
7. Place into the air fryer basket and cook for 10 minutes, turning midway through.
8. Serve and enjoy!

Soft- & Hard-Boiled Eggs

Boiled eggs in your air fryer? Of course! They're simple and delicious and make the perfect low carb breakfast or snack any time of day.

Serves: 6
Time: 20 mins
- Calories: 62
- Net carbs: 0g
- Protein: 5g
- Fat: 4g

Ingredients:
- 6 large free-range eggs

Method:
1. Preheat your air fryer to 250°F.
2. Place the eggs inside the basket then cook for 19 minutes (adjust the time according to how you like your eggs).
3. Remove from the air fryer and place into a bowl of cold water.
4. Serve and enjoy.

Cajun Breakfast Sausage

This Cajun breakfast is super easy when you use your air fryer. Perfectly low carb and delicious, it's perfect for long lazy weekends when you want to relax and enjoy something delicious. Add as much Tabasco sauce as you like to make the flavors really zing!

Serves: 13
Time: 45 mins
- Calories: 434
- Net carbs: 11g
- Protein: 11g
- Fat: 4g

Ingredients:
- 1 ½ lb. ground sausage
- 1 teaspoon chili flakes
- ½ teaspoon dried thyme
- 1 teaspoon onion powder
- ½ teaspoon paprika
- ½ teaspoon cayenne
- Salt and pepper, to taste
- Chopped sage (opt.)
- 2 teaspoons low carb sweetener
- 3 teaspoons minced garlic
- 2 teaspoon Tabasco sauce
- Herbs to garnish (opt.)

Method:
1. Preheat your air fryer to 370°F.
2. Grab a large bowl and add the sausage, herbs and spices. Stir well to combine.
3. Add as much Tabasco sauce as you like, stir again then shape into patties with your hands.
4. Place into the basket of your air fryer and cook for 20 minutes until crispy.
5. Serve and enjoy.

Cheese and Red Pepper Egg Cups

Looking for something special to start your day? Want to grab something and run? Create these delicious cheesy egg cups. Packed with antioxidants and healthy proteins, they'll get you fueled for anything!

Serves: 4
Time: 20 mins
- Calories: 195
- Net carbs: 7g
- Protein: 13g
- Fat: 12g

Ingredients:
- 4 large free-range eggs
- 1 cup diced red pepper
- 1 cup shredded cheese
- 4 tablespoons half and half
- 1 tablespoon chopped cilantro
- Salt and pepper, to taste

Method:
1. Preheat your air fryer to 300°F and grease four ramekins.
2. Grab a medium bowl and add the eggs. Whisk well.
3. Add the red pepper, half the cheese, the half and half, cilantro and the salt and pepper. Stir well to combine.
4. Pour the mixture between the ramekins and pop into the air fryer.
5. Cook for 12-15 minutes then serve and enjoy.

Breakfast Stuffed Peppers

Simple and perfectly delicious, these stuffed peppers will add a touch of spice and sweetness to your morning routine. For maximum nutrition, throw in a handful of baby spinach, spring onions and whatever else you fancy.

Serves: 2
Time: 25 mins

- Calories: 164
- Net carbs: 4g
- Fat: 11g
- Protein: 10g

Ingredients:

- 1 bell pepper halved, seeds removed
- 4 free-range eggs
- 1 teaspoon olive oil
- 1 pinch salt and pepper
- 1 pinch sriracha flakes (opt.)

Method:

1. Preheat your air fryer to 390°F.
2. Place the red pepper halves onto a flat surface and rub with olive oil.
3. Crack two eggs into each bell pepper half and sprinkle with salt, pepper and sriracha, if using.
4. Pop into the basket of your air fryer and cook for 13-15 minutes until cooked to perfection.
5. Serve and enjoy.

Sausage Breakfast Casserole

Sweet and nourishing peppers, fragrant onions and those breakfast basics hash browns, eggs and sausages come together in this low carb breakfast for the whole family. Omit the hash browns to slash the carb content even more.

Serves: 4
Time: 30 mins
- Calories: 768
- Net carbs: 41g
- Protein: 30g
- Fat: 53g

Ingredients:
- 1 lb. hash browns
- 1 lb. ground breakfast sausage
- 1 green bell pepper, diced
- 1 red bell pepper, diced
- 1 yellow bell pepper, diced
- ¼ cup sweet onion, diced
- 4 free-range eggs

Method:
1. Preheat your air fryer to 355°F.
2. Take the basket of your air fryer and line with foil.
3. Place the hash browns in the bottom followed by the sausage, the peppers and the onions.
4. Air fry for ten minutes then remove.
5. Crack the eggs onto the top of the hash brown mixture and pop back into the air fryer for 10 more minutes.
6. Serve and enjoy.

Pork

Pork Milanese

While you definitely DON'T have to make the arugula salad if you're not a fan of the peppery leaves, we highly recommend you do because they beautifully compliment the simple flavors of the pork. Yum!

Serves: 6
Time: 30 mins
- Calories: 485
- Net carbs: 7g
- Protein: 30g
- Fat: 34g

Ingredients:

For the pork...
- 6 center cut pork chops (about 4 oz. each)
- ½ cup flour
- 2 eggs, beaten with a splash of water
- 1 cup seasoned low carb bread crumbs
- 2 tablespoons olive oil

For the salad...
- 10 oz. fresh arugula
- 1 teaspoon Dijon mustard
- Juice of 1 lemon
- ½ cup olive oil
- ½ teaspoon salt
- Black pepper, to taste

Method:
1. Preheat air fryer to 390°F.
2. Place the pork chops onto a flat surface and cut into thin cutlets.
3. Grab a medium bowl and add the flour and the salt and pepper.
4. Take two other bowls, placing the egg into one and the breadcrumbs into the other.
5. Place the pork into the flour mixture and coat well.
6. Transfer to the egg mixture, allow any excess to drip off, then coat in the breadcrumbs.
7. Pop into the air fryer and cook for 5-6 minutes, turning midway through cooking.
8. Meanwhile, make the salad by placing the lemon, Dijon, salt and peppers into a bowl, and slowly adding the oil, stirring constantly.
9. Place the arugula and parmesan on top, toss then serve with the pork and enjoy.

Moroccan Style Pork Tenderloin

Take a trip over to North Africa with these deliciously fragrant, Moroccan-style pork tenderloins. Breathe in the heavenly scent and you can almost picture yourself there in the spice markets, surrounded by cinnamon, cayenne, paprika, coriander, ginger and many more besides. Enjoy!

Serves: 4
Time: 20 mins
- Calories: 650
- Net carbs: 13g
- Protein: 29g
- Fat: 20g

Ingredients:
- 2 ½ lb. pork tenderloins
- 1 teaspoon cumin
- ½ teaspoon cayenne pepper
- ¼ teaspoon ground cinnamon
- ½ teaspoon smoked paprika
- 1 tablespoon chili powder
- ¼ teaspoon ground coriander
- 1 teaspoon ground ginger to taste
- Salt and pepper, to taste
- ¼ cup olive oil
- 2-3 cloves garlic, smashed

Method:
1. Preheat your air fryer to 360°F
2. Grab a large bowl and add all the ingredients, except for the meat. Stir well to combine.
3. Add the meat and stir again to coat.
4. Place the pork into the air fryer and cook for 15 minutes.
5. Serve and enjoy.

Crispy Parmesan Crusted Pork Chops

If you love your pork to be spicy, you'll adore these chili parmesan pork chops. They're crunchy on the outside, tender on the inside and will keep you full and feeling fueled.

Serves: 4
Time: 20 mins
- Calories: 381
- Net carbs: 5g
- Protein: 42g
- Fat: 24g

Ingredients:
- 4 center-cut boneless pork chops
- ½ teaspoon salt
- ¼ teaspoon pepper
- 1 teaspoon smoked paprika
- ½ teaspoon onion powder
- ¼ teaspoon chili powder
- 2 large free-range eggs, beaten
- 1 cup pork rind crumbs
- 3 tablespoons grated parmesan cheese

Method:
1. Preheat your air fryer to 400°F.
2. Place the pork chops onto a flat surface and season with salt and pepper.
3. Grab your food processor and add the pork rinds. Blend until they form crumbs.
4. Place the crumbs into a large bowl with the seasoning and stir well to combine.
5. Grab a medium bowl and add the beaten eggs.
6. Take each pork chop and dip into the egg mixture, allow any excess to drip off then pop into the crumbs.
7. Cook for 15 minutes until delicious!
8. Serve and enjoy!

Cheesy Pork Chop Fries

Yes, you can even make fries using pork chops and they are AMAZING! Simply dressed in ranch dressing with a crunchy crust, they're awesome for a snack, main meal or post workout treat. Yum!

Serves: 4
Time: 25 mins

- Calories: 471
- Net carbs: 6g
- Protein: 57g
- Fat: 40g

Ingredients:

- 1 lb. pork chops, cut into fries
- ½ cup ranch dressing
- 1 x 3.5 oz. bag pork rinds, crushed into crumbs
- ½ cup parmesan cheese
- Salt and pepper, to taste

Method:

1. Preheat your air fryer to 380°F.
2. Place the pork chops onto a plate and season well with salt and pepper. Cut into fries.
3. Grab a medium bowl and add the ranch dressing.
4. Place the pork into the dressing and stir well to coat.
5. Open up your food processor and add the pork rinds and parmesan cheese. Whizz until fine.
6. Place these pork crumbs into a bowl and place the pork inside, coating well with breadcrumbs.
7. Pop into the air fryer and cook for 15 minutes, flipping part way through.
8. Serve and enjoy.

Pork Tonkatsu

Sometimes the simplest dishes work the best. That's certainly the case with this Japanese-inspired pork! Serve with whatever veggies your heart desires and fill your stomach with healthy goodness.

Serves: 2
Time: 20 mins

- Calories: 226
- Net carbs: 14g
- Protein: 12g
- Fat: 17g

Ingredients:

- 5 ½ oz. pork cutlet or boneless pork chop
- 1 free-range egg
- ½ cup panko
- ½ teaspoon salt
- ½ teaspoon pepper
- ½ teaspoon cayenne pepper, opt.

Method:

1. Preheat your air fryer to 360°F.
2. Find a medium bowl and combine the panko, salt, pepper and cayenne.
3. Take a smaller bowl and add the egg.
4. Place the pork into the egg, allow any excess to drip off then place into the breadcrumb mix.
5. Pop into your air fryer and cook for 10 minutes.
6. Serve and enjoy.

Memphis-Style BBQ Pork Ribs

If you're in the mood for pork ribs, make sure you give these incredible pork ribs a try. Made using the perfect combination of low carb spices, they'll create a meal to remember.

Serves: 6
Time: 40 mins
- Calories: 786
- Net carbs: 55g
- Protein: 30g
- Fat: 45g

Ingredients:
- 1 tablespoon salt (or to taste)
- 1 tablespoon sweetener
- 1 tablespoon sweet paprika
- 1 teaspoon garlic powder
- 1 teaspoon onion powder
- 1 teaspoon poultry seasoning
- ½ teaspoon mustard powder
- ½ teaspoon freshly ground black pepper
- 2 ¼ lb. individually cut St. Louis–style pork spareribs

Method:
1. Preheat the air fryer to 350°F.
2. Grab a large bowl and add the salt sugar, paprika, garlic, onion, poultry seasoning, mustard and pepper. Stir well to combine.
3. Place the ribs into the bowl and toss to coat.
4. Pop into the air fryer basket and cook for 35 minutes until crispy and delicious.
5. Serve and enjoy.

Chinese Salt and Pepper Pork Chops

This delicious dish will make you believe you're in a high-quality restaurant, but at a fraction of the calories of the cost. Teamed with a practically effortless stir fry, this dish comes together in less than 30 minutes, and tastes amazing.

Serves: 2
Time: 25 mins

- Calories: 451
- Net carbs: 53g
- Protein: 21g
- Fat: 16g

Ingredients:

For the pork...

- 2 pork chops, cut into pieces
- 1 egg white
- ½ teaspoon sea salt
- ¼ teaspoon black pepper
- ¾ cup potato starch
- Oil, to taste

For the veggies...

- 2 jalapeño pepper, stems removed, sliced
- 2 scallions, trimmed and sliced
- 2 tablespoons canola oil
- 1 teaspoon sea salt
- ¼ teaspoon black pepper

Method:

1. Preheat your air fryer to 360°F.
2. Grab a medium bowl and add the egg white, salt and pepper. Whisk until foamy.
3. Place pork pieces into the egg white mixture and stir well to coat.
4. Pop into the fridge for 20 minutes to marinade.
5. Place the potato starch into a bowl and add the pork pieces, stirring well to coat.
6. Spray the oil into the air fryer and cook for 10 minutes, stirring often.
7. Turn the air fryer up to 400°F then cook for a further 5 minutes until crispy.
8. Meanwhile, grab a wok or skillet, add oil and place over a high heat.
9. Add the jalapeno pepper, scallions, salt and pepper and stir fry for a minute.
10. Remove the pork from the air fryer and add to the jalapeno peppers, stirring well.
11. Serve and enjoy.

Rack of Lamb with Mint and Honey

Mmmm... the smell of roasting lamb takes me right back to my childhood where we enjoyed long and luxurious meals around the table, the conversation flowed, and I could eat my favorite food in the world. This air fryer version is just as delicious. Although honey isn't particularly low carb, I think it's well worth including. Feel free to switch for a sweetener of your choice.

Serves: 4
Time: 30 mins

- Calories: 662
- Net carbs: 8g
- Protein: 19g
- Fat: 64g

Ingredients:

- 2 racks of lamb
- 1 bunch fresh mint
- 2 garlic cloves, chopped
- ½ cup extra virgin olive oil
- 1 tablespoon honey
- Freshly ground pepper

Method:

1. Preheat your air fryer to 370°F.
2. Grab your food processor and add the honey, oil, garlic and mint. Whizz until smooth.
3. Place the lamb onto a flat surface and make small cuts around the racks so you can curl them into a circle.
4. Brush with the sauce you just made.
5. Pop into the air fryer and cook for 20 minutes.
6. Serve with extra mint sauce and enjoy!

Honey Mustard Pork Chops

These honey pork chops take the words 'fast food' to a whole new level. Thanks to your air fryer, they'll be ready in less than 15 minutes and they'll taste like you've been slaving away over them for hours.

Serves: 4
Time: 15 mins

- Calories: 138
- Net carbs: 9g
- Protein: 5g
- Fat: 14g

Ingredients:

- 4 pork chops, ½" thick
- 4 tablespoons mustard
- 2 tablespoons honey
- 2 tablespoons minced garlic
- 1 teaspoon salt
- 1 teaspoon pepper

Method:

1. Preheat the air fryer to 350°F.
2. Grab a large bowl and combine the mustard, honey, garlic, salt and pepper. Stir well.
3. Place the pork chops into the mustard mixture and stir well to coat.
4. Spray the air fryer basket then place the chops inside.
5. Air fry for 12 minutes until cooked, flipping often.
6. Serve and enjoy.

Cajun Cheese Pork Chops

I love cooking pork chops in my air fryer because I know that I can create something fast that hits all those nutritional bases and tastes amazing. You can't deny that the combo of almond flour, parmesan and Cajun spices makes your mouth water and your taste buds crave more.

Serves: 2
Time: 15 mins

- Calories: 431
- Net carbs: 3g
- Protein: 56g
- Fat: 20g

Ingredients:

- 2 boneless pork chops (1/2 lb. each)
- 1/3 cup almond flour
- 3 tablespoon grated parmesan cheese
- 1 teaspoon paprika
- 1 teaspoon Herbes de Provence
- 1 teaspoon Cajun seasoning

Method:

1. Preheat your air fryer to 350°F.
2. Take a medium bowl and add the almond flour, paprika, parmesan, herbs and other seasoning.
3. Spray your air fryer with oil then place the pork chops into the fryer basket.
4. Cook for 10 mins, turning often.

Pork Belly

Family dinners in my childhood home would never have been the same if it wasn't for the delicious, tender pork belly that my mother used to serve up. This fast air fryer version takes just a fraction of the time and tastes even better than the oven version. Bear in mind that it does take a couple of cooking steps, but don't be deterred. It's very much worth it!

Serves: 4
Time: 40 mins

- Calories: 594
- Net carbs: 2g
- Protein: 11g
- Fat: 60g

Ingredients:

- 1 lb. pork belly, cut into three
- 3 cups water
- 1 teaspoon salt
- 1 teaspoon pepper
- 2 tablespoons soy sauce
- 2 bay leaves
- 6 cloves garlic

Method:

1. Place all the ingredients into an Instant Pot or pressure cooker, cover with the lid and cook on manual high pressure for 15 minutes.
2. Do a natural pressure release for 10 minutes then quick release the remaining pressure.
3. Carefully remove the lid then transfer the pork to a place it can rest for 10 minutes.
4. Preheat your air fryer to 400°F then place the pork into the air fryer basket.
5. Cook for 15 minutes until crispy then serve and enjoy.

Scotch Eggs

Scotch eggs are a snack or picnic treat that hails from England and tastes AMAZING. With a hard-boiled egg at its core, a layer of pork sausage meat over the top, then a coating of cheesy, mustardy goodness, it's everything you could want in a low carb treat. Yum yum!

Serves: 4
Time: 45 mins
- Calories: 606
- Net carbs: 5g
- Protein: 43g
- Fat: 49g

Ingredients:
- 1 lb. pork sausage
- 1 tablespoon finely chopped fresh chives
- 2 tablespoons finely chopped fresh parsley
- 1/8 teaspoon freshly grated nutmeg
- 1/8 teaspoon salt
- 1/8 teaspoon ground black pepper
- 4 hard-cooked eggs, peeled
- 1 cup shredded parmesan cheese
- 2 teaspoons coarse-ground mustard

Method:
1. Preheat your air fryer to 400°F.
2. Meanwhile, grab a medium bowl and add the sausage, mustard, chives, parsley, nutmeg salt and pepper. Mix until combined.
3. Use your hands to shape into four patties.
4. Place a hard-boiled egg into the center of each patty and press the sausage mixture around the sides.
5. Roll the egg-sausage mixture in the parmesan until covered then place into the air fryer.
6. Cook for 15 minutes, stirring often.
7. Serve and enjoy.

Beef

Steak with Garlic Herb Butter

You've never tasted steak as good as these ones, I can almost guarantee it. Your air fryer will leave the steak perfectly tender and the homemade garlic butter will leave this dish lip-smackingly good. Enjoy!

Serves: 2
Time: 30 mins

- Calories: 683
- Net carbs: 23g
- Protein: 26g
- Fat: 30g

Ingredients:

- 2 x 8 oz. Ribeye steak, at room temperature
- Salt and pepper, to taste
- Olive oil, to taste
- 1 stick unsalted butter, softened
- 2 tablespoon fresh parsley, chopped
- 2 teaspoon garlic, minced
- 1 teaspoon Worcestershire sauce
- ½ teaspoon salt

Method:

1. Start by taking a small bowl and adding the butter, parsley, garlic, Worcestershire sauce and salt. Stir well until combined.
2. Place onto a piece of parchment paper and roll up until it forms a log. Pop into the fridge.
3. Preheat your air fryer to 400°F.
4. Pop the steak onto a flat surface, coat with oil, season with salt and pepper and pop into the air fryer.
5. Cook for 12 minutes, flipping halfway through.
6. Remove from the fryer, rest for 5 minutes then serve and enjoy.

Coffee & Spice Ribeye Steak

Sweet, tender and beautifully spiced, this steak dish will keep your carb count low without sacrificing a thing. Perfect for a romantic meal for two, it's a guaranteed winner. Again, don't be put off by the seemingly long list of spices in this recipe. It's definitely worth it!

Serves: 2
Time: 34 mins

- Calories: 495
- Net carbs: 5g
- Protein: 46g
- Fat: 32g

Ingredients:

- 1 lb. Ribeye steak, at room temperature
- 1 ½ teaspoon coarse sea salt
- 1 teaspoon sweetener
- ½ teaspoon ground coffee
- ½ teaspoon black pepper
- ¼ teaspoon chili powder
- ¼ teaspoon garlic powder
- ¼ teaspoon onion powder
- ¼ teaspoon paprika
- ¼ teaspoon chipotle powder
- 1/8 teaspoon coriander
- 1/8 teaspoon cocoa powder

Method:

1. Preheat your air fryer to 390°F.
2. Meanwhile, grab a medium bowl, add all the spices and stir well to combine.
3. Grab a flat dish and sprinkle with plenty of the spice mixture.
4. Pop the steaks into the spice mixture and stir well, pushing the spice mixture into the flesh.
5. Leave to rest for 10-20 minutes.
6. Spray your air fryer with some oil then place the steaks inside.
7. Cook for 10 minutes.
8. Remove and leave to rest for 5 minutes then serve and enjoy!

Carne Asada

Shhh! The secret of any awesome Carne Asada lies in the marinade. Find great quality ingredients, combine them with love and use your air fryer to cook it all to perfection and you'll have a melt-in-the-mouth dish that's packed with flavor. The leftovers are fab too.

Serves: 4
Time: 20 mins
- Calories: 330
- Net carbs: 1g
- Protein: 37g
- Fat: 19g

Ingredients:
For the steak...
- 1 ½ lb. skirt steak, cut into four

For the marinade...
- 2 medium limes, juiced
- 1 medium orange, peeled and seeded
- 1 cup cilantro
- 1 jalapeno, diced
- 2 tablespoons vegetable oil
- 2 tablespoons vinegar
- 2 teaspoons Ancho chili powder
- 1 teaspoon sweetener
- 1 teaspoon salt
- 1 teaspoon cumin seeds
- 1 teaspoon coriander seeds

Method:
1. Grab your blender and add all the marinade ingredients then whizz until smooth.
2. Place the steak into a large bowl and pour the marinade sauce over the top. Stir well to combine then pop into the fridge for 30 minutes.
3. Preheat your air fryer to 400°F.
4. Remove the steaks from the marinade and place into the air fryer.
5. Cook for 8-10 minutes until cooked.
6. Rest for 10 minutes then serve and enjoy!

Beef Satay

Spice up your life with this authentic but hands-off beef satay. Authentic, well-balanced but easy, you'll be licking your lips after you've whipped up this dish. Serve with peanuts or extra chopped cilantro for best flavor.

Serves: 4
Time: 45 mins
- Calories: 252
- Net carbs: 5g
- Protein: 14g
- Fat: 24g

Ingredients:
- 1 lb. beef flank steak, sliced thinly into long strips

To marinade…
- 2 tablespoons oil
- 1 tablespoon fish sauce
- 1 tablespoon soy sauce
- 1 tablespoon minced ginger
- 1 tablespoon minced garlic
- 1 tablespoon sugar
- 1 teaspoon Sriracha or other hot sauce
- 1 teaspoon ground coriander
- ¼ cup chopped cilantro

To serve…
- ¼ cup chopped roasted peanuts

Method:
1. Grab a medium bowl and add the marinade ingredients. Stir well.
2. Pop the beef into the marinade and stir well.
3. Pop into the fridge for 30 minutes to marinate.
4. Preheat your air fryer to 400°F.
5. Place the beef strips into the air fryer and cook for 8-10 minutes, turning midway through cooking.
6. Top with the peanuts plus extra cilantro then enjoy!

Beef Bulgogi Burgers

Who says that serving up burgers means that life has to get dull? Create these Asian-inspired burgers and you'll pack a flavorful punch whilst keeping life easy. Of course, you don't have to make the mayo if you're looking to cut down on calories, but these burgers just aren't the same without it.

Serves: 4
Time: 25 mins
- Calories: 392
- Net carbs: 7g
- Protein: 24g
- Fat: 29g

Ingredients:

For the Bulgogi Burgers…
- 1 lb. ground beef
- 2 tablespoon gochujang
- 1 tablespoon dark soy sauce
- 2 teaspoons minced garlic
- 2 teaspoons minced ginger
- 2 teaspoons sugar
- 1 tablespoon sesame oil
- ¼ cup green onions
- ½ teaspoon salt

For the mayo…
- ¼ cup mayo
- 1 tablespoon gochujang
- 1 tablespoon sesame oil
- 2 teaspoons sesame seeds
- ¼ cup scallions, chopped

Method:
1. Grab a large bowl and add the burger ingredients.
2. Stir well then leave to rest for 30 minutes into the fridge.
3. Preheat your air fryer to 360°F.
4. Use your hands to divide into four and gently push your finger into the center to help the burgers keep their shape.
5. Place into the air fryer and cook for 10 minutes.
6. Meanwhile, make the mayo by combining the mayo ingredients in a bowl and stirring well.
7. Serve together and enjoy!

Bourbon Bacon Burger

OK, so you might have taken a look at this recipe and thought, "WHAT? That's not easy!!" But I promise you that it absolutely is! Take it step by step and you'll make a truly unforgettable burger with a difference. Besides, you can just skip certain bits if you want, although we wouldn't advise it!

Serves: 4
Time: 40 mins
- Calories: 326
- Net carbs: 12g
- Protein: 20g
- Fat: 26g

Ingredients:

For the bacon...
- 1 tablespoon bourbon
- 1 tablespoon sweetener
- 3 strips maple bacon, cut in half

For the burgers...
- ¾ lb. ground beef
- 1 tablespoon minced onion
- 2 tablespoons BBQ sauce
- ½ teaspoon salt
- Black pepper, to taste

To serve...
- 2 slices Colby Jack cheese (or Monterey Jack)
- 2 low carb rolls
- Lettuce and tomato, for serving

For the sauce...
- 2 tablespoons BBQ sauce
- 2 tablespoons mayonnaise
- ¼ teaspoon ground paprika
- Freshly ground black pepper

Method:
1. Preheat your air fryer to 390°F.
2. Grab a small bowl and combine the sweetener and bourbon. Stir well.
3. Place the bacon into the sugar mixture and stir well to coat.
4. Pop into the air fryer and cook for 8 minutes, flipping half way through cooking and brushing with extra sugar if required.

5. Meanwhile, grab a medium bowl and add the burger ingredients. Stir well until everything is combined.
6. Shape into four patties and push a finger gently into the middle to help the burgers keep their shape.
7. Turn the air fryer down to 370°F and cook the burgers for 15-20 minutes, until cooked through.
8. Make the mayo by combining all the mayo ingredients in a small bowl and stirring well.
9. Serve everything together and enjoy!

Beef Steak Kebabs

All it takes is a quick 30-minute marinade and you can transform average steak into soy-spiked, juicy and tender kebabs which simply melt in your mouth. Try it! You'll see.

Serves: 4
Time: 40 mins
- Calories: 250
- Net carbs: 4g
- Protein: 23g
- Fat: 6g

Ingredients:
- 1 lb. beef chuck ribs cut in 1" pieces
- 1/3 cup low fat sour cream
- 2 tablespoon soy sauce
- 8 x 6" skewers
- 1 bell peppers, cut into chunks
- ½ onion, cut into chunks

Method:
1. Take a medium bowl and add the soy sauce and sour cream. Stir well.
2. Place the beef into a bowl and marinade for 30 minutes, longer if you can.
3. Soak the skewers in water for 10 minutes, then remove from the water.
4. Preheat your air fryer for 400°F.
5. Carefully push the beef onto the skewer, alternating with the pepper and onion pieces.
6. Season well with pepper then place into your air fryer.
7. Cook for 10 minutes, turning midway through cooking.

Rib Eye Steak with Blue Cheese Butter

There's something about blue cheese which adds a certain zing and intensity of flavor to your average steak. We love it! That's why we always make time to eat this super-fast, ultra-easy steak meal. Not only does it taste amazing, but it also keeps us fueled for hours.

Serves: 2
Time: 15 mins

- Calories: 829
- Net carbs: 2g
- Protein: 69g
- Fat: 60g

Ingredients:

- 2 x 12 - 16 oz. Rib eye steaks, 1" thick
- 1-2 teaspoons salt
- 1 ½ teaspoons black pepper
- 1 teaspoon garlic powder

For the blue cheese butter...

- 1 stick butter, at room temperature
- 4 oz. blue cheese of choice

Method:

1. Grab a small bowl and add the blue cheese. Mash well with a fork then add the butter. Stir well until well combined and smooth. Pop into the fridge until needed.
2. Preheat your air fryer to 400°F.
3. Place the steaks on to a flat surface and season with salt, pepper and garlic powder, covering well.
4. Cook the steaks for 7-8 minutes, flipping halfway through.
5. Leave to rest for a minute or two before removing from the air fryer.
6. Serve with the blue cheese butter and enjoy!

Beef Lasagna

Yes, you can even make a filling beef lasagna using the powers of your air fryer. It's much less hassle than cooking a lasagna in your oven and it will be ready in a fraction of the time.

Serves: 4
Time: 30 mins
- Calories: 838
- Net carbs: 10g
- Protein: 62g
- Fat: 65g

Ingredients:

For the Meat Layer…
- Olive oil
- 1 lb. 85% ground beef
- 1 cup prepared marinara sauce
- ¼ cup diced celery
- ¼ cup diced red onion
- ½ teaspoon minced garlic
- Salt and pepper

For the cheese layer…
- 8 oz. ricotta cheese
- 1 cup shredded cheese, divided
- ½ cup grated parmesan cheese
- 2 large free-range eggs
- 1 teaspoon dried Italian seasoning
- ½ teaspoon minced garlic

For the topping…
- Grated mozzarella, to taste

Method:
1. Preheat your air fryer to 375°F and grease a pan that will fit into your air fryer.
2. Take a large bowl and add the ingredients for the meat layer. Stir well to combine.
3. Place the meat into the pan, spreading evenly.
4. Pop into the air fryer and cook for 10 minutes.
5. Meanwhile, take another bowl and add the cheese layer ingredients. Stir well.
6. Remove the pan from the air fryer and add the cheese mixture.
7. Spread well then top with the mozzarella. Pop into the air fryer again.
8. Cook for 10 minutes then remove and leave to rest for 5 minutes.
9. Serve and enjoy.

Keto Steak Nuggets

Steak nuggets are even better than chicken nuggets, especially when you coat them in low carb breadcrumbs, air fry them to perfection and serve them with a dip this good. Who needs takeout when you have these??

Serves: 4
Time: 50 mins

- Calories: 609
- Net carbs: 2g
- Protein: 63g
- Fat: 38g

Ingredients:

For the steak...

- 1 lb. steak, cut into chunks
- 1 large free-range egg

For the breadcrumbs...

- ½ cup grated parmesan cheese
- ½ cup pork panko
- ½ teaspoon homemade seasoned salt

For the chipotle ranch dip...

- ¼ cup mayonnaise
- ¼ cup sour cream
- 1 teaspoon chipotle paste (or to taste)
- ½ teaspoon My Ranch Dressing & Dip Mix
- ¼ medium lime, juiced

Method:

1. Start by making the dip. Grab a medium bowl and add the dip ingredients. Mis well then pop into the fridge until needed.
2. Next take another medium bowl and add the panko, parmesan and salt. Stir well.
3. Take another medium bowl, add the egg and beat well.
4. Dip the steak into the egg, allow any excess to drip off then dip into the breadcrumb mixture.
5. Pop onto a lined baking tray and pop into the freezer for 30 minutes. This will help the breadcrumbs to stick better during cooking.
6. Preheat the air fryer to 370°F and cook the steak pieces for 8-10 minutes, turning often.
7. Serve with the dip and enjoy!

Chicken and Turkey

Baked Chicken Nuggets with Crunchy Almond Dip

What did we just say about chicken nuggets? We take it all back! These are amazing too. Coated in crunchy, calcium-rich sesame seeds, they'll light up your taste buds and keep your carb count in check. The dip is pretty good too...

Serves: 4
Time: 25 mins
- Calories: 286
- Net carbs: 13g
- Protein: 11g
- Fat: 18g

Ingredients:
- 1 lb. chicken breast, cut into nuggets
- Pinch sea salt
- 1 teaspoon sesame oil
- ¼ cup coconut flour
- ½ teaspoon ground ginger
- 4 egg whites
- 6 tablespoons toasted sesame seeds

For the dip...
- 2 tablespoons almond butter
- 4 teaspoons soy sauce
- 1 tablespoon water
- 2 teaspoons rice vinegar
- 1 teaspoon Sriracha, or to taste
- ½ teaspoon ground ginger
- ½ teaspoon Monk fruit sweetener (or alternative)

Method:
1. Preheat your air fryer to 400°F.
2. Place the chicken pieces into a bowl and add the salt and sesame seeds. Stir well until the chicken is coated.
3. Next grab a medium bowl and add the coconut flour and ginger. Stir well then pour over the chicken.
4. Take a medium bowl and add the egg whites, whisking well.
5. Place the chicken nuggets into the egg white mixture and stir well until coated.
6. Spray the air fryer with oil then place the chicken inside.
7. Cook for 12-15 minutes until perfectly cooked.
8. Serve with the dip and enjoy!

BBQ Chicken Wings

How easy do you want dinner to be?? These chicken wings combine everything that is delicious about chicken and lovingly coats it in a garlicky, spiced coating. Mmmm....

Serves: 4

Time: 25 mins

- Calories: 330
- Net carbs: 35g
- Protein: 2g
- Fat: 18g

Ingredients:

- 1 ¾ lb. chicken wings
- 1 teaspoon garlic powder
- 1 teaspoon smoked paprika
- Salt and pepper, to taste
- 1 teaspoon olive oil
- 2 tablespoons barbecue sauce (or to taste)

Method:

1. Preheat the air fryer to 360°F.
2. Grab a large bowl and add the garlic powder, paprika, salt and pepper. Stir well.
3. Add the oil and stir again, then place the chicken wings inside. Stir again to coat.
4. Place the chicken into the air fryer basket and cook for 12 minutes, flipping often.
5. Remove from the fryer and place back into the bowl.
6. Add the barbeque sauce, stir well then place back into the air fryer.
7. Cook for a further 2-3 minutes then serve and enjoy.

Buffalo Chicken Legs

If you've just got your hands on your air fryer, we recommend you kick-start your journey with these super-easy, super-tasty chicken legs. They're finger-lickin' good and you can make them as spicy as you like!

Serves: 4
Time: 30 mins

- Calories: 476
- Net carbs: 0g
- Protein: 30g
- Fat: 50g

Ingredients:

- 2 lb. chicken drumsticks, skin removed
- 2 tablespoons butter, melted
- ¼ cup hot sauce

Method:

1. Preheat the air fryer to 400°F.
2. Spray the air fryer with oil then cook the drumsticks for 20 minutes, flipping midway through cooking.
3. Place the butter and hot sauce in a bowl, stir well then add the cooked chicken. Stir well to coat then return to the air fryer.
4. Cook for a further 5 minutes until crispy.
5. Serve and enjoy!

Chicken Coconut Meatballs

Combining tender, melt-in-the-mouth chicken and tender coconut, these meatballs are low carb, healthy and eye-poppingly good. Packed full of Asian goodness, they're perfect for serving with a simple side of cabbage or low-carb noodles.

Serves: 4
Time: 25 mins

- Calories: 223
- Net carbs: 3g
- Protein: 20g
- Fat: 14g

Ingredients:

- 1 lb. ground chicken
- 2 green onions, finely chopped
- ½ cup cilantro, chopped
- 1 tablespoon Hoisin sauce
- 1 tablespoon soy sauce
- 1 teaspoon Sriracha
- 1 teaspoon sesame oil
- ¼ cup unsweetened shredded coconut
- Salt and pepper, to taste

Method:

1. Preheat your air fryer to 350°F.
2. Grab a large bowl and add all the ingredients. Stir well together.
3. Using your hands, shape into meatballs and pop into the air fryer.
4. Cook for 10 minutes, turning midway through cooking.
5. Serve and enjoy.

Jalapeno Popper Stuffed Chicken Breast

It's always hard to pick which is the best part of these jalapeno popper chicken breasts. Could it be the creamy cream cheese, the feisty cheddar, the salty bacon or the spice of the jalapenos themselves? Who knows! All I know is that it's one of my favorite dishes in the entire world!

Serves: 4
Time: 30 mins
- Calories: 654
- Net carbs: 2g
- Protein: 62g
- Fat: 42g

Ingredients:
- 4 x 4 oz. chicken breasts, butterflied
- 2 jalapeños
- 4 oz. cream cheese
- 4 oz. cheddar cheese
- 8 strips bacon

Method:
1. Preheat your air fryer to 370°F.
2. Place the chicken onto a flat surface and spread the inside with cream cheese.
3. Add half the jalapenos to each chicken breast and top with the cheddar cheese.
4. Close the chicken then wrap with two slices of bacon.
5. Cook for 20 minutes, turning often.
6. Serve and enjoy.

Bagel Chicken Roll-Ups

You can't go wrong with these bagel chicken roll ups. Packed with cheese and spinach goodness and the perfect amount of seasoning, you can whip these up fast and have them on the table before your appetite has even kicked in properly.

Serves: 8 (2 roll ups each)
Time: 30 mins

- Calories: 397
- Net carbs: 4g
- Protein: 53g
- Fat: 16g

Ingredients:

- 2 large egg whites
- ½ cup whipped cream cheese
- ½ cup shredded cheddar cheese
- ¼ cup chopped scallions
- 8 chicken breast cutlets, thin-sliced
- ½ cup chopped baby spinach
- Olive oil spray

For the bagel seasoning…

- 2 tablespoons dried minced onion
- 2 tablespoons dried minced garlic
- 2 tablespoons poppy seeds
- ½ cup + 1 tablespoon white sesame seeds
- 1 tablespoon black sesame seeds
- 1 tablespoon coarse salt

Method:

1. Preheat your air fryer to 375°F.
2. Grab a shallow bowl and add the bagel seasoning ingredients. Stir well to combine.
3. Take another bowl and add the egg white, whisking well.
4. Find another bowl and add the cream cheese, cheddar and scallions. Mix well to combine.
5. Place the chicken onto a flat surface, spread some of the cheese mixture into the middle, place the spinach onto the top then roll up.
6. Pop onto a plate, seam side down.
7. Dip each of the rolls into the egg whites, allow any excess to drip off then drag through the seasoning.
8. Cook for 15 minutes, turning halfway through.

Tandoori Chicken

You'd be forgiven for thinking that tandoori chicken is challenging to make. But nothing could be further from the truth, even if you're a complete beginner. Just throw the marinade into a bowl, stir well, and you're practically done.

Serves: 4
Time: 45 mins
- Calories: 178
- Net carbs: 2g
- Protein: 25g
- Fat: 6g

Ingredients:
- 1 lb. chicken tenders, each cut in half
- ¼ cup Greek yogurt
- 1 tablespoon minced ginger
- 1 tablespoon minced garlic
- ¼ cup cilantro or sub parsley
- 1 teaspoon salt
- ½ – 1 teaspoon cayenne pepper
- 1 teaspoon turmeric
- 1 teaspoon garam masala
- 1 teaspoon sweet smoked paprika
- 1 tablespoon oil

To serve…
- 2 teaspoons lemon juice
- 2 tablespoons chopped cilantro

Method:
1. Grab a medium bowl and combine all the ingredients except the oil. Stir well.
2. Preheat your air fryer to 350°F.
3. Brush the chicken with the oil then coat with the spice mixture.
4. Place into the air fryer and cook for 30 minutes or until cooked through, turning often.
5. Serve and enjoy.

Spicy Mexican Chicken Burgers

Beautifully spiced with cayenne, mustard and plenty of herbs, these low carb burgers will satisfy even the biggest of appetites! They're perfect for any gathering, big or small and will nourish you from the inside out. The combo of cauliflower 'breadcrumbs' and spices is also epic.

Serves: 4
Time: 45 ins

- Calories: 240
- Net carbs: 14g
- Protein: 32g
- Fat: 7g

Ingredients:

- 4 chicken breasts, skin and bones removed
- 1 small cauliflower
- 1 free-range egg, beaten
- 3 tablespoons smoked paprika
- 1 tablespoon dried thyme
- 1 tablespoon oregano
- 1 tablespoon mustard powder
- 1 teaspoon cayenne pepper
- 1 jalapeno pepper
- Salt & pepper, to taste

Method:

1. Preheat the air fryer to 350°F.
2. Grab your blender and add the cauliflower and the seasoning. Whizz until it looks like breadcrumbs.
3. Place ¾ of the breadcrumbs into to a bowl and the remaining ¼ into another bowl.
4. Add the egg to the ¼ portion and stir well. Pop to one side.
5. Take your blender again and add the chicken and ¼ of the cauliflower and seasoning mixture. Season well then whizz again.
6. Using your hands, form into patties.
7. Dip the patties into the beaten egg mixture then toss in the remaining seasoned cauliflower.
8. Cook in the air fryer for 30 minutes, turning halfway through.
9. Serve and enjoy.

Easy Piri-Piri Chicken

You can never go wrong with piri-piri! Perhaps it's the European in me, but I love this dish so much that appears on our dinner menu at least once per week. Did I mention that it's also quick, easy and nourishing too?

Serves: 4
Time: 40 mins
- Calories: 510
- Net carbs: 19g
- Protein: 35g
- Fat: 62g

Ingredients:
- 1 whole chicken
- 1 ½ cup olive oil
- 5/8 cup low carb tomato sauce
- 1 tablespoon garlic puree
- 1 tablespoon paprika
- 1 tablespoon fresh parsley
- 1 tablespoon Piri Piri seasoning
- Salt & pepper, to taste

Method:
1. Preheat your air fryer to 350°F.
2. Place your chicken onto a sheet of foil.
3. Grab your blender and add the remaining ingredients then hit whizz.
4. Brush the sauce over the chicken and season well, then wrap in the foil.
5. Pop into the freezer for an hour.
6. Place the package into your air fryer and cook for 25 minutes, turning halfway through cooking.
7. Remove from the air fryer then unwrap the chicken.
8. Serve and enjoy.

Adobo Air Fried Chicken Thighs

Another beginner friendly recipe, this delicious chicken dish is crunchy, low carb and unforgettable. Make it now!

Serves: 4
Time: 25 mins
- Calories: 359
- Net carbs: 1g
- Protein: 36g
- Fat: 24g

Ingredients:
- 4 large chicken thighs
- 2 tablespoons adobo seasoning
- 1 tablespoon olive oil

Method:
1. Preheat your air fryer to 350°F.
2. Pop the chicken onto a flat surface and brush with oil.
3. Place the adobo seasoning into a medium bowl and add the chicken, stirring well to coat.
4. Place into the air fryer and cook for 20 minutes, turning often.
5. Serve and enjoy.

Spicy Popcorn Chicken

Lightly spiced, tender and perfectly crunchy, this popcorn chicken is a dish you'll want to make again and again, especially if you have a crowd to serve. You can play around and get creative with the coating ingredients to find the right combination for you.

Serves: 6-8
Time: 25 mins

- Calories: 105
- Net carbs: 12g
- Protein: 15g
- Fat: 6g

Ingredients:

- 1 lb. boneless skinless chicken tenderloins or chicken breasts, cut into bite-sized pieces
- 1 tablespoon honey or low carb sweetener
- 1 teaspoon black pepper
- 1 teaspoon garlic powder
- 1 teaspoon ground mustard
- 1 teaspoon paprika
- ¼ teaspoon salt
- 2 cups unfrosted cornflakes

Method:

1. Preheat the air fryer to 400°F.
2. Grab a small bowl and add the spices. Stir well to combine.
3. Add the honey to the bowl and stir again, then pop to one side.
4. Find a medium bowl and add the cornflakes. Crush well using the end of a rolling pin.
5. Place the chicken into the honey-spice mix and stir well to coat.
6. Roll in the crushed cornflakes then place into the air fryer.
7. Cook for 10-14 minutes, turning halfway through.
8. Serve and enjoy.

Italian Chicken Tenders

Next time you want a taste of Italy, dive into the kitchen and create these scrumptious chicken tenders. They're fast, they're delicious and they're ready in the blink of an eye- perfect for weeknights when you can't be bothered to cook but still want something nutritious to eat.

Serves: 4
Time: 20 mins
- Calories: 448
- Net carbs: 47g
- Protein: 15g
- Fat: 36g

Ingredients:
- 1 ½ lb. chicken tenders
- 2 free-range eggs
- 1 cup fine almond flour
- 2 tablespoons ground flax seed
- 1 teaspoon Italian seasoning
- 1 teaspoon fine sea salt
- 1 teaspoon paprika
- ½ teaspoon ground black pepper
- ½ teaspoon garlic powder
- ½ teaspoon onion powder

Method:
1. Preheat your air fryer to 400°F.
2. Place the chicken onto a flat surface and season well with salt and pepper.
3. Take a medium bowl and add the eggs, whisking well.
4. Find a shallow dish and add the almond flour, flax and all the seasonings. Stir well until combined.
5. Take the chicken and dip into the egg, allowing any excess to drip off.
6. Place into the flour and coat well.
7. Place into your air fryer and cook for 15 minutes, turning midway though.
8. Serve and enjoy.

Easy Low Carb Turkey Meatballs

Light, melt-in-the-mouth and utterly moreish, these meatballs come together fast to make an easy meal that will feel the whole family. Low carb and healthy, they also pack a protein punch and keep you feeling nourished.

Serves: 8
Time: 20 mins
- Calories: 451
- Net carbs: 6g
- Protein: 33g
- Fat: 32g

Ingredients:
- 1 lb. turkey
- 1 lb. turkey sausage
- ¼ cup onion, minced
- 2 cloves garlic, minced
- 2 tablespoons parsley, chopped
- 2 free-range eggs
- 1 ½ cup parmesan cheese, grated
- Salt and pepper, to taste

Method:
1. Preheat your air fryer to 350°F.
2. Place all the ingredients into a medium bowl and stir well to combine.
3. Use your hands to form into meatballs.
4. Cook for 13 minutes, turning midway through cooking.
5. Serve and enjoy!

Sage and Rosemary Fried-Turkey Wings

These sage and rosemary turkey wings will show you that turkey can be scrumptious, even if you've never been much a fan of it. Tender, fragrant and very moreish, they're perfect to share and amazing when served with lightly sautéed veggies.

Serves: 4
Time: 40 mins

- Calories: 568
- Net carbs: 9g
- Protein: 48g
- Fat: 39g

Ingredients:

- 2 lb. turkey wings
- 3 tablespoons olive oil or sesame oil (or less, to taste)
- 1 teaspoon dried thyme
- 1 teaspoon dried rosemary
- 1 teaspoon fresh or dry sage, chopped
- Salt and pepper, to taste

Method:

1. Preheat your air fryer to 380°F.
2. Place the turkey wings onto a flat surface and brush with oil.
3. Take a small bowl and add the thyme, rosemary, sage and seasonings. Stir well to combine.
4. Rub the herbs into the skin of the turkey then pop into the air fryer basket.
5. Cook for 25 minutes, flipping halfway through.
6. Remove from the air fryer then serve and enjoy.

Turkey Breast

You'll be amazed to see just how well turkey breast turns out when roasted in the air fryer. Moist, perfectly cooked and delicious, it stores brilliantly if you have leftovers so you can get meal prepping for the week ahead. Double win!

Serves: 10
Time: 1 hour

- Calories: 226
- Net carbs: 0g
- Protein: 33g
- Fat: 10g

Ingredients:

- 4 lb. turkey breast, on the bone with skin (ribs removed)
- 1 tablespoon olive oil
- 2 teaspoons kosher
- ½ tablespoon dry turkey or poultry seasoning

Method:

1. Preheat your air fryer to 350°F.
2. Place the turkey on a flat surface and rub the olive oil over the flesh.
3. Season with salt and pepper then place into the air fryer.
4. Cook for 30-40 minutes until cooked through.
5. Remove from the air fryer and leave to rest for 10 minutes.
6. Serve and enjoy.

Lamb

Simple Lamb Chops

Combine mustard, tarragon and olive oil with a touch of lemon and you can absolutely rock these lamb chops. Better still, they only take 20 minutes in your air fryer so you can have dinner on the table fast. Awesome!

Serves: 4
Time: 20 mins
- Calories: 254
- Net carbs: 8g
- Protein: 7g
- Fat: 18g

Ingredients:
- 8 loin lamb chops, 1 ¼" wide
- 2 tablespoons mustard Dijon or whole grain
- ½ teaspoon olive oil
- 1 teaspoon tarragon
- 1 tablespoon lemon juice
- Salt and pepper, to taste

Method:
1. Preheat your air fryer to 390°F.
2. Grab a small bowl and add the mustard, olive oil, tarragon and lemon juice. Stir well.
3. Place the lamb onto a flat surface and brush with the mustard mixture.
4. Pop into the air fryer and cook for 20 minutes, turning half way through.
5. Serve and enjoy.

Lamb and Spinach Meatballs with Tzatziki

Spinach is a wonderful source of iron and works brilliantly when teamed with feta cheese, oregano and garlic. That's why I love to make these meatballs. They're nourishing, very easy and taste even better when teamed with this effortless tzatziki. Yummy!

Makes: 30 meatballs
Time: 30 mins
- Calories: 486
- Net carbs: 50g
- Protein: 21g
- Fat: 30g

Ingredients:
- 1 ½ lb. ground lamb
- 2 cups packed chopped spinach
- 2 cloves minced garlic
- 1 cup minced onion
- 1/3 cup chopped pine nuts
- 1 tablespoon finely minced fresh oregano
- ½ teaspoon salt
- ½ cup finely crumbled feta
- 1 free-range egg
- 2 tablespoons olive oil

For the Tzatziki...
- 1 cup full-fat plain Greek yogurt
- 1/3 cup diced cucumber
- 2 tablespoons chopped fresh dill
- 2 tablespoons chopped fresh mint
- 2 teaspoons lemon juice
- 1 teaspoon olive oil
- 1-2 cloves garlic
- ¼ teaspoon salt

Method:
1. Grab a skillet, add the oil and place over a medium heat.
2. Add the onion and cook for 5-10 minutes until soft.
3. Add the garlic and cook for another minute or two, then throw in the spinach. Remove from the heat.

4. Place the spinach mixture into a large bowl and add the meatball ingredients. Stir well.
5. Using your hands, shape into meatballs.
6. Cook in the air fryer for 10-15 minutes, turning often.
7. Meanwhile, take a medium bowl and combine the tzatziki ingredients in a small bowl and mix thoroughly.
8. Serve and enjoy.

Moroccan Lamb Burgers

These burgers are soo good that I'd eat them every day if I had to, especially when teamed with lashings of spicy sauce. Serve with a large salad and enjoy!

Serves: 4
Time: 20 mins
- Calories: 478
- Net carbs: 3g
- Protein: 28g
- Fat: 38g

Ingredients:

For the burgers...
- 1 ½ lb. minced lamb
- 2 teaspoons garlic puree
- 1 teaspoon harissa paste
- 1 tablespoon Moroccan spice
- Salt & pepper, to taste

For the burger sauce...
- 3 tablespoons Greek yoghurt
- 1 teaspoon Moroccan spice
- ½ teaspoon oregano
- Juice of one small lemon

Method:
1. Preheat your air fryer to 360°F.
2. Grab a medium bowl and add all the ingredients, stirring well to combine.
3. Using your hands, form into patties, gently pressing in the middle to help them hold their shape.
4. Pop into the air fryer and cook for 18-20 minutes, flipping halfway through.
5. Meanwhile, take a medium bowl and add the sauce ingredients. Stir well.
6. Serve and enjoy.

Rosemary and Garlic Rack of Lamb

You've never tasted anything as good as this rosemary and garlic lamb! Moist, fragrant and nourishing, it's everything that you want your rack of lamb to be but without any of the hassle. Just 20 minutes is all you need to make a dish this good.

Serves: 2
Time: 20 mins

- Calories: 827
- Net carbs: 97g
- Protein: 37g
- Fat: 37g

Ingredients:

- 1 rack of lamb
- 2 tablespoons dried rosemary
- 1 tablespoon dried thyme
- 2 teaspoons minced garlic
- Salt and pepper, to taste
- 4 tablespoons olive oil

Method:

1. Preheat your air fryer to 360°F.
2. Take a small bowl and add the rosemary, thyme, garlic, salt, pepper and olive oil. Stir well to combine.
3. Place the lamb on a flat surface and rub the herb mixture into the flesh.
4. Pop into the air fryer and cook for 10 minutes.
5. Serve and enjoy!

Mojito Lamb Kabobs

Find yourself the juiciest limes, the freshest mint and the biggest cloves of garlic and I promise you won't want to make anything else all week! Bear in mind that you do need a couple of hours to marinate these guys, but I promise that it's well worth the wait.

Serves: 4
Time: 45 mins
- Calories: 696
- Net carbs: 12g
- Protein: 65g
- Fat: 22g

Ingredients:
- 3 limes, zested and juiced
- ½ cup olive oil
- ¼ cup fresh mint, chopped
- 8 large cloves garlic, minced
- 2 teaspoons salt
- ½ teaspoon pepper
- 12 lamb loin chops, trimmed

Method:
1. Grab a medium bowl and add the lime juice and zest, the mint, garlic, salt, pepper and oil. Stir well to combine.
2. Place the lamb into the bowl and stir well to coat.
3. Cover and pop into the fridge for at least 4 hours, preferably overnight.
4. Preheat your air fryer to 370°F.
5. Place the lamb into the air fryer and cook for 20-30 minutes until cooked to perfection.
6. Serve and enjoy!

Lamb Kofta Kabab

This lamb kofta kebab recipe is so effortless and so good, you're bound to want to make it again and again and again! Combining fragrant kofta spice with the most tender lamb, it delivers a ton of nutrients in a healthy, low carb package.

Serves: 4
Time: 30 min

- Calories: 279
- Net carbs: 4g
- Protein: 21g
- Fat: 20g

Ingredients:

- 1 tablespoon oil
- 1 lb. ground beef
- ¼ cup chopped parsley
- 1 tablespoon minced garlic
- 2 tablespoons kofta kabab spice mix
- 1 teaspoon salt

Method:

1. Grab a large bowl and add all the ingredients. Stir well to combine.
2. Cover and pop into the fridge for at least 30 minutes, overnight if you can.
3. Preheat your air fryer to 370°F.
4. Shape the mixture into meatball shapes using your hands and pop into the air fryer basket. You can also use skewers if you want to be more authentic.
5. Cook for 10 minutes then serve and enjoy.

Fish and Seafood

Tuna Patties

Grab a bunch of herbs, combine them with flaky, rich tuna and air fry them to perfection. Yes, that's all you need to do to create a super-fast, healthy meal for two or even a special brunch. Enjoy!

Serves: 2
Time: 15 mins
- Calories: 580
- Net carbs: 6g
- Protein: 18g
- Fat: 35g

Ingredients:
- 2 cans tuna, packed in water
- 1 ½ tablespoons almond flour
- 1 ½ tablespoons mayo
- 1 teaspoon dried dill
- 1 teaspoon garlic powder
- ½ teaspoon onion powder
- Pinch of salt and pepper
- Juice of ½ lemon

Method:
1. Preheat your air fryer to 400°F.
2. Grab a large bowl and add all the ingredients. Stir well to combine.
3. Using your hands, form into patties. Feel free to add extra flour if they feel too sticky.
4. Pop into your air fryer and cook for 10-13 minutes.
5. Serve and enjoy.

Thai Fish Cakes

Close your eyes and take a bite of these beauties and you'll believe that you're right there in Thailand, sunning yourself on the beach and enjoying a taste of heaven. Tender, beautifully spiced and almost effortless, these fish cakes are amazing.

Serves: 4
Time: 30 mins
- Calories: 352
- Net carbs: 0g
- Protein: 4g
- Fat: 27g

Ingredients:
- 1 lb. barramundi filets skin removed, cut into 1" pieces
- 3 tablespoons coconut butter
- 3 tablespoons fish sauce
- 2 tablespoons water
- 2 cloves garlic
- 1 tablespoon grated fresh ginger
- 1 tablespoon fresh cilantro leaves
- ½ teaspoon chili powder
- ½ teaspoon red pepper flakes
- ½ teaspoon ground cumin
- ¼ teaspoon ground coriander
- 2 tablespoons coconut oil
- Lime wedges

For the spicy mayo…
- 3 tablespoons mayonnaise
- ½ to 1 teaspoon hot sauce or Sriracha

Method:
1. Preheat your air fryer to 400°F.
2. Grab a large bowl and combine all the ingredients. Stir well.
3. Using your hands, shape into patties then pop into your air fryer.
4. Cook for 10-13 minutes.
5. Serve and enjoy.

Crispy Fish Sticks

Imagine you could take those dull, premade fish fingers, wave a magic wand over them and create something that gourmet chefs would be proud of. Yes, that's how good these fish sticks are. Coating in a gorgeous combination of pork rink and Cajun spices, they're crunchy, flaky and far too moreish.

Serves: 4
Time: 20 mins

- Calories: 263
- Net carbs: 1g
- Protein: 26g
- Fat: 16g

Ingredients:

- 1 lb. white fish such as cod, cut into sticks 1" x 2"
- ¼ cup mayonnaise
- 2 tablespoons Dijon mustard
- 2 tablespoons water
- 1 ½ cups pork rind panko such as Pork King Good
- ¾ teaspoon Cajun seasoning
- Salt and pepper, to taste

Method:

1. Preheat your air fryer to 400°F.
2. Take a small bowl and combine the mayo, mustard and water. Stir well.
3. Take a shallow dish and add the Cajun spices and pork rinds. Season to taste.
4. Grab a cod stick and dip first into the mayo then into the pork rind mixture.
5. Cook in the air fryer for 10 minutes, flipping midway through.

Coconut Shrimp

Coconut and shrimp- what an effortlessly brilliant team! You'll never want to cook your shrimp any other way when you've tried these. Yum!

Serves: 4
Time: 25 mins
- Calories: 191
- Net carbs: 16g
- Protein: 13g
- Fat: 6g

Ingredients:
- ¼ cup cornstarch
- 1 teaspoon salt
- 2 egg whites
- 1 cup flakes sweetened coconut
- ½ lb. large raw shrimp

Method:
1. Preheat the air fryer to 330°F.
2. Grab a shallow dish and add the corn starch and salt.
3. Take another dish and add the egg whites, mixing well.
4. Take yet another dish and add the coconut.
5. Dip the shrimp into the corn starch, then the egg then the coconut.
6. Pop into the air fryer and cook for 15 minutes.
7. Serve and enjoy.

Curried Salmon Cakes

The secret to these lightly spiced salmon cakes lies in popping them into the freezer. Just 30 minutes is all you need to have a crunchy-yet-tender salmon cake that will please the whole family. Delicious!

Serves: 4
Time: 50 mins
- Calories: 519
- Net carbs: 22g
- Protein: 22g
- Fat: 28g

Ingredients:
- 1 lb. salmon, diced
- ¼ cup avocado, mashed
- ¼ cup cilantro, diced + additional for garnish
- 1 ½ teaspoon yellow curry powder
- ½ teaspoon salt
- ¼ cup + 4 teaspoon tapioca starch, divided
- 2 free-range eggs
- ½ cup coconut flakes
- Coconut oil, melted

For the salad…
- 6 cups arugula & spinach mix, tightly packed

Method:
1. Grab a large bowl and add the salmon, avocado, curry and salt and stir well.
2. Add 4 tablespoons of tapioca starch and stir again.
3. Using your hands, form the salmon into patties then place onto a prepared baking sheet and pop into the freezer for 20 minutes.
4. Preheat the air fryer to 400°F.
5. Take a shallow dish and add the eggs, whisking well to combine.
6. Take another plate and add the coconut and the rest of the tapioca starch.
7. Remove the salmon cakes from the freezer and dip into the eggs then the coconut mixture.
8. Pop into the air fryer and cook for 15 minutes, turning often.
9. Meanwhile, pop the coconut oil into a skillet and place over a medium heat.
10. Add the arugula and spinach, season and cook for 1 minutes.
11. Remove from the heat and divide between the four plates.
12. Top with the salmon cakes then enjoy!

Perfect Air Fryer Salmon

Salmon cooked in the air fryer is a real revelation. Packed with healthy omega-3 oils, it will be ready super-fast and taste beautifully simple. What more do you need for a healthy, low carb meal?

Serves: 2
Time: 12 mins

- Calories: 287
- Net carbs: 1g
- Protein: 18g
- Fat: 28g

Ingredients:

- 2 salmon fillets
- 2 teaspoons olive oil
- 2 teaspoons paprika
- Salt and pepper, to taste
- Lemon wedges

Method:

1. Preheat your air fryer to 390°F.
2. Bring the salmon to room temperature for an hour then brush with olive oil and season with paprika, salt and pepper.
3. Place into the air fryer then cook for 7 minutes.
4. Serve and enjoy.

Cilantro Lime Air Fryer Shrimp

The uplifting yet earthy flavors of cumin, garlic, cilantro and lime come together to make this shrimp burst with flavor. If you'd prefer not to use a skewer then feel free to ditch it and serve with a simple green salad instead.

Serves: 4
Time: 20 mins

- Calories: 60
- Net carbs: 3g
- Protein: 11g
- Fat: 8g

Ingredients:

- ½ lb. raw shrimp, peeled and deveined
- ½ teaspoon garlic purée
- ½ teaspoon paprika
- ½ teaspoon ground cumin
- Juice of 1 lemon
- Salt, to taste
- 1 tablespoon chopped cilantro

Method:

1. Grab 6 wooden skewers and pop them into a dish of water to soak.
2. Preheat your air fryer to 350°F.
3. Take a medium bowl and add the lemon, garlic, paprika, cumin and salt. Stir well.
4. Add the shrimp and stir again to coat.
5. Remove the skewers from the water and carefully thread the shrimp onto them.
6. Pop into the air fryer and cook for 8 minutes, turning often.
7. Serve and enjoy.

Parmesan Shrimp

Whenever I sink my teeth into this parmesan shrimp, I'm transported to the Mediterranean where I can soak up the sunshine and enjoy the simple life, simple food and great company. That's why I love making these on a dull winter's day- they're guaranteed to inject some sunshine into your life!

Serves: 4
Time: 15 mins
- Calories: 479
- Net carbs: 5g
- Protein: 25g
- Fat: 82g

Ingredients:
- 2 lb. jumbo cooked shrimp, peeled and deveined
- 4 cloves garlic, minced
- 2/3 cup parmesan cheese, grated
- 1 teaspoon pepper
- ½ teaspoon oregano
- 1 teaspoon basil
- 1 teaspoon onion powder
- 2 tablespoons olive oil
- Lemon, quartered

Method:
1. Preheat your air fryer to 350°F.
2. Take a medium bowl and add the parmesan, garlic, pepper, oregano, basil, onion and olive oil. Stir well to combine.
3. Add the shrimp and stir well.
4. Place the shrimp into the air fryer and cook for 10 minutes.
5. Serve and enjoy.

Cajun Crispy Golden Fish

This wonderful crispy Cajun fish will melt in your mouth, fall off your fork and leave your taste buds dancing with delight. If you're not keen on catfish you can substitute for whatever fish your heart desires. Yum!

Serves: 2
Time: 20 mins
- Calories: 212
- Net carbs: 9g
- Protein: 35g
- Fat: 3g

Ingredients:
- 2 tablespoons cornmeal polenta
- 2 teaspoons Cajun seasoning
- ½ teaspoon paprika
- ½ teaspoon garlic powder
- Salt, to taste
- 2 catfish fillets

Method:
1. Preheat your air fryer to 400°F.
2. Grab a medium bowl and add all the ingredients except the fish. Stir well to combine.
3. Add the fish and stir well until coated.
4. Pop into the air fryer and cook for 15 minutes, flipping half way through.
5. Serve and enjoy!

Vegetarian & Vegan

Lupini Falafal

These falafal are a wonderful low carb side dish, main or even snack that everyone can enjoy- whether they're following a plant-based diet or not. Simply delicious!

Serves: 4

Time: 38 mins

- Calories: 188
- Net carbs: 12g
- Fat: 12g
- Protein: 5g

Ingredients:

- 1 cup brined lupini beans (soaked in hot water for 60 mins)
- 1 ½ cups thawed frozen broccoli
- ¼ cup tahini
- 2 tablespoons lemon juice
- 1 tablespoon dried parsley
- 2 teaspoons cumin
- 2 tablespoons ground chia seeds
- ½ teaspoon garlic powder
- ¼ teaspoon onion powder
- ¼ teaspoon all spice

Method:

1. Preheat your air fryer to 350°F.
2. Grab your food processor and add the beans and broccoli. Whizz until they're very finely chopped.
3. Pop into a medium bowl and add the tahini, lemon juice and seasoning. Stir well to combine.
4. Add the chia seeds, stir again then leave to rest for 5 minutes.
5. Using your hands, form into patties and place into your air fryer.
6. Cook for 15 minutes then serve and enjoy.

Super Crispy Air Fryer Tofu

Using just a handful of ingredients, this tofu is transformed into something utterly memorable! For best results, make sure you press as much of the liquid out of the tofu before you get started.

Serves: 4
Time: 15 mins
- Calories: 63
- Net carbs: 4g
- Fat: 1g
- Protein: 7g

Ingredients:
- 14 oz. (1 block) extra firm tofu
- 1 tablespoon corn starch
- 1 teaspoon smoked paprika
- ½ teaspoon ground coriander
- Sea salt, to taste

Method:
1. Preheat your air fryer to 400°F.
2. Grab a medium bowl and add the corn starch, the spices and the salt. Stir well to combine.
3. Add the tofu and stir well until coated.
4. Pop the tofu into the air fryer and cook for 12-15 minutes until perfect.
5. Serve and enjoy.

Vegan Mini Veggie Burritos

Crunchy on the outside, tender and delicious on the inside, these burritos are packed with flavor and nutrition. You can throw in whatever veggies you have lying around to make a treat to remember. Wow!

Serves: 4
Time: 30 mins
- Calories: 198
- Net carbs: 23g
- Fat: 10g
- Protein: 11g

Ingredients:
- 2 tablespoons cashew butter
- 2 - 3 tablespoons tamari
- 1- 2 tablespoons liquid smoke
- 1-2 tablespoons water
- 4 pieces rice paper
- 2 servings tofu (scrambled to taste)

Optional extras…
- ⅓ cup roasted sweet potato cubes
- 8 strips roasted red pepper
- 1 small head broccoli, sautéed
- 6-8 stalks fresh asparagus
- Handful spinach, kale, or other greens

Method:
1. Preheat the air fryer to 350°F.
2. Take a shallow dish and mix together the cashew butter, tamari, liquid smoke and water. Pop to one side.
3. Gather together whatever extra ingredients you want to use.
4. Fill a shallow dish with water and place a rice paper sheet inside until wet.
5. Remove and place onto a plate then fill with the ingredients.
6. Roll up, seal then dip into the cashew butter sauce.
7. Repeat with the remaining sheets of rice paper then place inside the air fryer.
8. Air fry for 10-15 minutes until crisp.
9. Serve and enjoy.

Tofu Satay with Peanut Butter Sauce

Who knew that tofu could taste so good? Bathed in a sweet, sticky and spicy marinade then served with a crunchy and delicious peanut butter sauce, it's a dish that will surprise and delight. The original recipe contains maple syrup but feel free to switch for low carb sweetener if you want to keep the carb count lower.

Serves: 4
Time: 40 mins
- Calories: 163
- Net carbs: 11g
- Fat: 4g
- Protein: 3g

Ingredients:
- 2 tablespoons soy sauce
- Juice of 1 fresh lime
- 1 tablespoon maple syrup or sweetener
- 2 teaspoons fresh ginger, coarsely chopped
- 1 teaspoon sriracha sauce
- 2 cloves garlic, chopped
- 1 block tofu, cut into strips

For the peanut butter sauce…
- 2-3 tablespoons peanut butter
- Water to thin the sauce

Method:
1. Grab your blender and add the soy sauce, lime juice, maple syrup, ginger, sriracha and garlic. Whizz until smooth.
2. Pour into a medium bowl, add the tofu and stir to coat.
3. Cover and pop into the fridge for 30 minutes.
4. Preheat your air fryer to 370°F and soak 6 wooden skewers in water.
5. Remove the tofu from the fridge and remove the skewers from the water.
6. Carefully threat the tofu onto each skewer and pop into the air fryer.
7. Cook for 15 minutes.
8. Meanwhile, find a small bowl and combine the peanut butter with enough water to make a sauce. Adjust the quantities to make the sauce perfect for your tastes.
9. Serve and enjoy.

Ginger Tofu Sushi Bowl

The star of the show has to be the ginger-sesame tofu which has been air fried to perfection. Piled onto your favorite selection of tender rice, crunchy veggies and Asian condiments, it's beautiful dish that competes with anything you'd find in a restaurant. Wow!

Serves: 4
Time: 50 mins
- Calories: 485
- Net carbs: 35g
- Fat: 17g
- Protein: 14g

Ingredients:

For the tofu...
- 2" piece fresh ginger
- 1 clove garlic
- 2 tablespoons maple syrup
- 1 tablespoon toasted sesame oil, opt
- 2 tablespoons soy sauce
- 1 teaspoon rice vinegar
- 1 tablespoon corn starch
- 1 block extra firm tofu, pressed and cut into 1" pieces

For the sushi bowl...
- 3 cups cooked rice
- ½ cup carrot sticks
- ¾ cup cucumber, sliced into 1/4" thick half-moons
- 1 Haas avocado sliced

Optional toppings...
- 1 x 16 oz. package roasted seaweed snacks, cut into thirds
- ¼ cup pickled ginger, opt.
- ½ cup roasted cashews
- 1 green onion, chopped

Method:
1. Grab your blender and add the ginger, garlic, maple syrup, sesame oil, soy sauce and vinegar. Whizz until smooth.
2. Pour into a medium bowl, add the tofu and stir well to coat.
3. Cover and pop into the fridge for 30 minutes.
4. Preheat your air fryer to 375°F

5. Remove the tofu from the marinade then toss in the corn starch.
6. Pop into the air fryer for 15 minutes, turning halfway through.
7. Serve with the rice, avocado, carrots, cucumbers and whatever other topping you desire.
8. Enjoy!

Asian Vegetable Spring Rolls

Switch up your meals by taking a bite of these mouth-wateringly crunchy spring rolls. Containing the perfect balance of veggies and seasonings, they're a low carb vegetarian option that's great for any occasion.

Serves: 8
Time: 45 mins

- Calories: 80
- Net carbs: 10g
- Protein: 3g
- Fat: 1g

Ingredients:

For the filling...

- 2 cups shredded cabbage
- 1 large carrot, grated
- 1 onion, sliced
- ½ bell pepper
- 2" fresh ginger
- 8 cloves garlic
- Pinch sweetener
- 1 tablespoon ground pepper
- 1 teaspoon soy sauce
- Spring onion, to garnish
- Oil, for frying

For the wrap...

- 1 teaspoon soy sauce
- 2 tablespoons oil
- Spring onion, to garnish
- 10 sheets spring roll sheet
- 2 tablespoons corn flour
- Water, as needed

Method:

1. Preheat your air fryer to 350°F.
2. Grab a large bowl and add the filling ingredients. Stir well to combine.
3. Pop a wok over a high heat and add some of the oil.
4. Throw the veggies into the wok and cook for 5 minutes.
5. Remove from the heat, add a pinch of the sweetener and stir well to combine.
6. Take a small bowl and add the corn flour and just enough water to make a paste.

7. Place a wrap onto a flat surface and cut into half.
8. Pop a small amount of filling into one corner of each and roll up tightly.
9. Seal using a small amount of the corn flour paste then pop to one side.
10. Repeat with the remaining rolls.
11. Place into your air fryer and cook for 20 minutes until perfect.
12. Serve and enjoy.

Broccoli Tofu Scramble

Whether you're looking for a delicious breakfast, easy light lunch or summer, you'll love this broccoli and tofu scramble. Rich in iron, calcium and vitamin C plus a ton of plant-based protein, it will fill your tummy and fuel you for anything!

Serves: 2-4
Time: 40 mins
- Calories: 348
- Net carbs: 61g
- Protein: 15g
- Fat: 8g

Ingredients:
- 1 block tofu, chopped into 1" pieces
- 2 tablespoons soy sauce
- 2 tablespoons olive oil
- 1 teaspoon turmeric
- ½ teaspoon garlic powder
- ½ teaspoon onion powder
- ½ cup chopped onion
- 2-3 potatoes, chopped into small pieces (opt.)
- 4 cups broccoli florets

Method:
1. Preheat your air fryer to 400°F.
2. Grab a large bowl and add the tofu, half of the olive oil, turmeric, garlic powder, onion powder and onion. Stir well.
3. Add the soy sauce and stir again.
4. If eating potatoes, take a medium bowl and combine the potatoes and the remaining olive oil. Stir well then pop into the air fryer for 15 mins.
5. Remove the potatoes from the air fryer and pop to one side.
6. Now add the tofu to the air fryer, turn the temperature down to 370°F and cook for 15 minutes.
7. Return the potatoes to the air fryer, add the broccoli and cook for a further 5 minutes.
8. Serve and enjoy.

Crunchy Panko Tofu

Take yourself back to Asia with this crunchy, delicious tofu dish. Honestly, we like to just serve it and eat it as it is, or with a side of pickled ginger and other treats. Fast and delicious, everyone in the family will love this recipe.

Serves: 4

Time: 30 mins

- Calories: 272
- Net carbs: 26g
- Fat: 8g
- Protein: 11g

Ingredients:

- 1 block extra firm tofu, pressed and sliced into 8 cutlets
- ½ cup vegan mayo
- 1 cup panko breadcrumbs
- 1 teaspoon sea salt

For the marinade…

- 1 tablespoon toasted sesame oil
- ¼ cup soy sauce
- 1 teaspoon rice vinegar
- ½ teaspoon garlic powder
- 1 teaspoon ground ginger

Method:

1. Grab a medium bowl and add the sesame oil, soy sauce, vinegar, garlic and ginger. Stir well to combine.
2. Add the tofu, stir well then cover and pop into the fridge for 30 minutes.
3. Preheat the air fryer to 370°F.
4. Meanwhile, place the mayo into a shallow bowl and place the panko and salt together in another bowl.
5. Remove the tofu from the fridge and allow any excess marinade to drip off.
6. Dip into the mayo, then the panko, then transfer to the air fryer.
7. Cook for 20 minutes, shaking often.
8. Serve and enjoy!

Thai Veggie Bites

The first time I ever made the gorgeous veggie bites was for a friend's birthday party, and I tell you, they went down a treat! Even though I made several batches, they were snatched up before anything else and enjoyed by all present. Perfect as a snack, lunch or dinner, they also keep brilliantly in the fridge, making them perfect for meal planning too.

Makes: 16 bites
Time: 25 mins
- Calories: 117
- Net carbs: 9g
- Fat: 7g
- Protein: 2g

Ingredients:

The veggies....
- 1 large head broccoli, chopped
- 1 large head cauliflower, chopped
- 6 large carrots, chopped
- Handful garden peas

For the onion base...
- 1 large onion, peeled and diced
- 1 small zucchini, sliced
- 2 leeks, cleaned and thinly sliced
- 1 can coconut milk
- ½ cauliflower, made into cauliflower rice

The spices...
- 2 oz. all-purpose flour
- ½ inch cube ginger, peeled and grated
- 1 tablespoon garlic puree
- 1 tablespoon olive oil
- 1 tablespoon Thai Green Curry paste
- 1 tablespoon coriander
- 1 tablespoon mixed spice
- 1 teaspoon cumin
- Salt & pepper, to taste

Method:
1. Pop your veggies (except the zucchini and leek) into a steamer and cook for around 20 minutes until perfect.
2. Grab a wok, add the olive oil and place over a medium heat.
3. Add the onion and cook for five minutes until soft.
4. Next add the garlic and ginger, stir well and cook for another minute until fragrant.
5. Add the zucchini and leek and stir well.
6. Throw in the curry paste and coconut milk and stir again.
7. Add the rest of the seasonings, along with the cauliflower rice. Cook for 10 minutes until reduced by half.
8. Stir through the steamed veggies then leave to cool for an hour, or longer if you can.
9. Preheat your air fryer to 350°F.
10. Using your hands, press into patties and place into your air fryer.
11. Cook for 10 minutes then serve and enjoy!

Portobello Mushroom Pizzas

Even vegans can enjoy 'pizza', as you'll see with these amazing mushroom pizzas. You can pile up whatever topping your like then leave all the effort to your air fryer for a perfectly balanced, earthy and delicious vegan snack or meal.

Serves: 4
Time: 25 mins

- Calories: 70
- Net carbs: 11g
- Fat: 2g
- Protein: 4g

Ingredients:

- 4 large Portobello mushrooms, cleaned
- Balsamic vinegar, as needed
- Salt and black pepper, to taste
- 4 tablespoons pasta sauce
- 1 clove garlic, minced
- 3 oz. zucchini, shredded
- 2 tablespoons sweet red pepper, diced
- 4 Kalamata olives, sliced
- 1 teaspoon dried basil
- ½ cups hummus

Method:

1. Preheat the air fryer to 330°F.
2. Cut off the stems of the portobellos and remove the gills.
3. Spray with balsamic vinegar and season well.
4. Spread a tablespoon of pasta sauce into each mushroom and sprinkle with garlic.
5. Place into the air fryer and cook for 3 minutes then remove and place on a flat surface.
6. Top the mushrooms with peppers, zucchini and olives, sprinkle with basil, season again and return to the air fryer.
7. Cook for a further 3 minutes.
8. Remove from the air fryer, drizzle with hummus then serve and enjoy!

Thai-Style Vegan Crab Cakes

You'll never believe that these crab cakes are vegetarian friendly once you've tried them. Combining an ingenious selection of palm hearts, artichokes, potatoes and delicious Thai flavors, you'll know that you're nourishing your body with less carbs and less fat than you could ever believe. Yum!

Serves: 4-6
Time: 35 mins
- Calories: 97
- Net carbs: 20g
- Fat: 0.4g
- Protein: 4g

Ingredients:
- 4 cups diced potatoes
- 7-8 green onions
- 1 lime, zest & juice
- 1½" fresh ginger
- 1 tablespoon tamari or soy sauce
- 4 tablespoons Thai Red Curry Paste
- 4 sheets Nori, broken into pieces
- 1 can hearts of palm, drained and shredded
- ¾ cup canned artichoke hearts
- Salt and pepper, to taste
- 2 tablespoons oil

Method:
1. Grab a pan of boiling water and add the potatoes. Cook until soft.
2. Drain the potatoes, mash well then pop to one side to cool.
3. Meanwhile, grab your food processor and add the green onions, lime juice and zest, ginger, tamari, nori and curry paste. Whizz until smooth.
4. Add the curry paste, hearts of palm and artichoke to the potatoes and stir well to combine.
5. Preheat your air fryer to 400°F.
6. Use your hands to form into patties and then place into your air fryer.
7. Cook for 10-15 minutes until perfectly crisp.
8. Serve and enjoy!

Cauliflower Chickpea Tacos

I love how easy this taco recipe is! Boasting the perfect blend of spices, quickly air fried, wrapped in soft and delicious tortillas and topped with a delicious blend of avocado, cabbage and vegan yoghurt, you'll definitely want to make these again. Tip: The cauliflower and chickpea mixture also work well if you're making a large salad to share.

Serves: 4

Time: 30 mins

- Calories: 403
- Net carbs: 15g
- Fat: 14g
- Protein: 16g

Ingredients:

- 4 cups cauliflower florets, cut into bite-sized pieces
- 19 oz. can chickpeas, drained and rinsed
- 2 tablespoons olive oil
- 2 tablespoons taco seasoning

To serve...

- 8 small low carb tortillas
- 2 avocados, sliced
- 4 cups cabbage, shredded
- Coconut yogurt to drizzle

Method:

1. Preheat your air fryer to 390°F.
2. Grab a large bowl and add the cauliflower, chickpeas, olive oil and taco seasoning. Stir well to combine.
3. Transfer to the basket of your air fryer and cook for 20 minutes.
4. Serve with the avocado, cabbage and yoghurt.
5. Enjoy!

Side Dishes

Crispy Balsamic Brussels Sprouts

Give your Brussels sprouts a facelift with your air fryer! All you need is a dash of olive oil, balsamic vinegar and salt and you can transform then from 'meh...' to 'WOW!'.

Serves: 2
Time: 15 mins

- Calories: 107
- Net carbs: 12g
- Protein: 8g
- Fat: 2g

Ingredients:

- 2 cups halved Brussels sprouts, sliced in half lengthwise
- 1 tablespoon olive oil
- 1 tablespoon balsamic vinegar
- ¼ teaspoon sea salt

Method:

1. Preheat your air fryer to 400°F.
2. Grab a bowl and combine the sprouts, oil, vinegar and salt. Stir well to combine.
3. Pop into the air fryer and cook for 10 minutes.
4. Serve and enjoy.

Maple Syrup Bacon

Once you've tried this bacon, you'll never eat it any other way! Simple and delicious, it works perfectly as a side, as a salad topping, as a snack or even as a sandwich filling. Switch the maple syrup for a mix of sweetener and water if you're looking to lower the carbs even further.

Makes: 11 slices
Time: 10 mins
- Calories: 91
- Net carbs: 0g
- Protein: 8g
- Fat: 2g

Ingredients:
- 11 slices thick cut bacon
- Maple syrup (or sweetener), to taste

Method:
1. Preheat your air fryer to 400°F.
2. Place the bacon on the flat surface and brush with the maple syrup.
3. Transfer to the air fryer and cook for 10 minutes.
4. Serve and enjoy!

Fried Asparagus with Spicy Mayo Dip

When you want a treat yourself to something special, why not create this amazing side dish. I often make it just to enjoy as finger-food with my loved ones or as a low carb snack with drinks.

Serves: 2
Time: 25 mins
- Calories: 420
- Net carbs: 7g
- Protein: 9g
- Fat: 40g

Ingredients:
- 10 fresh asparagus spears, trimmed
- Vegetable oil

For the egg wash...
- 1 large free-range egg
- 1 tablespoon heavy whipping cream

For the breading...
- 1/3 cup blanched almond flour
- 1/3 cup finely grated parmesan cheese
- ½ teaspoon salt
- ½ teaspoon paprika

For the dip...
- ¼ cup mayonnaise
- 1 teaspoon Dijon mustard
- ¼ teaspoon cayenne
- ¼ teaspoon black pepper

Method:
1. Preheat the air fryer to 400°F.
2. Grab a small bowl and add all the ingredients for the dip. Stir well to combine then pop into the fridge.
3. Grab a shallow dish and add the egg and cream. Whisk together.
4. Take another shallow dish and add the breading ingredients, stirring well until combined.
5. Dip the asparagus into the egg mixture, allow any excess to drip off then roll in the breadcrumbs.
6. Place into the air fryer and cook for 5-10 minutes until perfect.
7. Serve and enjoy!

Feta Psiti Greek Baked Feta

Who knew that feta cheese could taste this good???

Serves: 6
Time: 30 mins
- Calories: 161
- Net carbs: 3g
- Protein: 14g
- Fat: 5g

Ingredients:
- 8 oz. feta cheese
- ¼ cup red onion, sliced thin
- ¼ cup red pepper, chopped
- 1 small jalapeno pepper
- 12 pitted cherry tomatoes, cut in half
- 10 whole Kalamata olives, minced
- 2 cloves fresh garlic, minced
- 1 teaspoon dried oregano
- ½ teaspoon Sambal Oelek ground chili paste (or other chili paste, to taste)
- 2 ½ tablespoons olive oil, divided

Method:
1. Preheat your air fryer to 300°F.
2. Grab a medium bowl and add all the ingredients except the olive oil and feta. Stir well to combine.
3. Add 2 tablespoons of oil and stir again.
4. Add the feta and stir again.
5. Place the feta mixture into your air fryer and cook for 10 minutes.
6. Leave to rest inside the air fryer for 5 minutes then serve and enjoy.

Avocado Fries

I didn't even realize it was possible to make avocado fries until my sister treated me to a batch a couple of years back. They're a perfect way to enjoy firm avocados and they taste beautiful! Enjoy!

Serves: 4
Time: 13 mins
- Calories: 308
- Net carbs: 17g
- Protein: 24g
- Fat: 10g

Ingredients:
- 1 cup low carb flour
- 1 cup low carb breadcrumbs
- 2 free-range eggs
- 2 tablespoons water
- 4 avocados, sliced into wedges (firm is good)
- Seasonings, to taste

Method:
1. Preheat your air fryer to 400°F.
2. Take a shallow dish and combine the flour, breadcrumbs, and seasonings. Stir well.
3. Grab another bowl and add the eggs and the water. Whisk together.
4. Dip the avocado wedges into the egg mixture, then into the breadcrumb mixture.
5. Pop into the air fryer and cook for 8-10 minutes
6. Serve and enjoy.

Onion Rings

There's nothing in this world like homemade onion rings, especially when you know they're low carb and easy. Perfect for parties, gatherings or just a healthy snack, they're tasty, easy and wonderful.

Serves: 4
Time: 26 mins

- Calories: 172
- Net carbs: 5g
- Protein: 1g
- Fat: 15g

Ingredients:

- 1 onion, sliced
- 1 ¼ cup flour
- 1 teaspoon baking powder
- 1 free-range egg, beaten
- 1 cup + 1 teaspoon milk
- ¾ cup breadcrumbs
- Seasonings

Method:

1. Preheat your air fryer to 370°F.
2. Grab a medium bowl and add the flour, baking powder and seasonings. Stir well to combine.
3. Take a shallow dish and add the egg and milk. Whisk together.
4. Dip a slice of onion into the egg mixture, then into the breadcrumbs.
5. Pop into the air fryer and cook for 8-10 minutes.
6. Serve and enjoy.

Roasted Asian Broccoli

Although this broccoli is a side dish, I often just make a huge batch and tuck right in. Packed with nourishing vitamins, minerals and antioxidants, it's an Asian treat flecked with peanuts, soy, honey and garlic.

Serves: 4
Time: 30 mins
- Calories: 154
- Net carbs: 22g
- Protein: 8g
- Fat: 11g

Ingredients:
- 1 lb. broccoli, cut into florets
- 1 ½ tablespoons peanut oil
- 1 tablespoon garlic, minced
- Salt, to taste
- 2 tablespoons soy sauce
- 2 teaspoons honey
- 2 teaspoons Sriracha
- 1 teaspoon rice vinegar
- 1/3 cup roasted salted peanuts
- Fresh lime juice (opt.)

Method:
1. Preheat your air fryer to 400°F.
2. Grab a large bowl and add the broccoli, peanut oil, garlic and seasoning. Stir well to combine.
3. Place into the air fryer and cook for 15 minutes.
4. Serve and enjoy.

Air Fryer Fried Pickles

I've always loved pickles, but I never thought they could taste this good. Coated in pork rind and cheese, you get that perfect crunch before you sink your teeth in for that bite. Wow!

Serves: 4
Time: 15 mins

- Calories: 245
- Net carbs: 0g
- Protein: 17g
- Fat: 17g

Ingredients:

- ½ cup crushed pork rinds
- 3 tablespoons parmesan cheese, finely grated
- 16 sliced dill pickles
- ½ cup almond flour
- 1 large free-range egg, beaten
- 1 teaspoon olive oil

Method:

1. Preheat the air fryer to 370°F.
2. Take a shallow dish and add the pork and parmesan. Stir well to combine.
3. Take another bowl and add the egg. Whisk well.
4. Take another bowl and add the almond flour.
5. Dip the pickle in the almond flour, then the egg, then the pork and parmesan.
6. Cook for 6 minutes.
7. Serve and enjoy.

Bacon and Cream Cheese Stuffed Jalapeno Poppers

Quick, spicy and fantastic for those snacking moments, these jalapeno poppers will set your mouth on fire whilst soothing your taste buds with their creamy bacon goodness. Yum!

Serves: 5
Time: 15 mins

- Calories: 62
- Net carbs: 13g
- Protein: 9g
- Fat: 10g

Ingredients:

- 10 fresh jalapenos, sliced in half horizontally
- 6 oz. cream cheese, softened in the microwave
- ¼ cup shredded cheddar cheese
- 2 slices bacon

Method:

1. Preheat your air fryer to 370°F.
2. Grab a medium bowl and add the cream cheese, bacon and shredded cheese. Stir to combine.
3. Place the jalapenos onto a flat surface and fill with the cheese mixture.
4. Transfer to the air fryer and cook for 10-15 minutes.
5. Serve and enjoy.

Cauliflower Buffalo Wings

What else do you need in a side dish?? Cauliflower, buffalo sauce and a dip into your air fryer and you have an excellent side dish or tasty snack to keep those taste buds happy.

Serves: 4
Time: 20 mins
- Calories: 101
- Net carbs: 7g
- Protein: 3g
- Fat: 7g

Ingredients:
- 1 head cauliflower, cut into pieces
- ½ cup buffalo sauce
- 1 tablespoon butter
- Salt and pepper, to taste

Method:
1. Preheat the air fryer to 400°F.
2. Grab a medium bowl and add the butter, buffalo sauce and salt and pepper. Stir well to combine then pop to one side
3. Pop the cauliflower into the air fryer and cook for 7 minutes.
4. Remove the cauliflower from the air fryer and add to the butter mixture. Stir to coat.
5. Pop into the air fryer again and cook for another 7 minutes.
6. Serve and enjoy.

Healthy French Fries

OK, so these French fries aren't exactly low carb in the traditional sense of the word, but they are much healthier than the regular kind. Still, we thought they were worth including in this book. Enjoy!

Serves: 4
Time: 30 mins

- Calories: 585
- Net carbs: 120g
- Protein: 5g
- Fat: 16g

Ingredients:

- 3 medium russet potatoes, cut into ¼" fries
- 2 tablespoons Parmesan cheese
- 2 tablespoons finely chopped fresh parsley
- 1 tablespoon olive oil
- Salt, to taste

Method:

1. Preheat the air fryer to 360°F.
2. Place the potatoes into a large bowl and add the cheese, herbs and oil. Stir well.
3. Transfer to the air fryer and cook for 20 mins, turning often.
4. Serve and enjoy.

Healthy Zucchini Corn Fritters

Every vegetarian will LOVE these corn fritters because they're not just fritters, they're almost a meal in themselves! Packed with veggies, they keep the carb count low whilst tasting incredible. Enjoy!

Serves: 4
Time: 22 mins

- Calories: 107
- Net carbs: 19g
- Protein: 3g
- Fat: 2g

Ingredients:

- 2 medium zucchinis, shredded
- 1 cup corn kernels
- 1 medium potato, cooked and smashed
- 2 tablespoons chickpea flour
- 2-3 garlic finely minced
- 1-2 teaspoon olive oil
- Salt and pepper, to taste

To serve...

- Ketchup or Yogurt tahini sauce

Method:

1. Preheat the air fryer to 360°F.
2. Grab a large bowl and add all the ingredients. Stir well to combine.
3. Using your hands, form into patties and place into your air fryer.
4. Cook for 12-15 minutes, turning halfway through.
5. Serve with the ketchup or yoghurt tahini sauce.

Eggplant Parmesan

Next time you create an Italian meal, make sure you whip up a quick side dish or starter of these delicious treats. Topped with a delicious crust and melty mozzarella, they take everything that is awesome about the Med and make it even better.

Serves: 4

Time: 40 mins

- Calories: 193
- Net carbs: 24g
- Protein: 6g
- Fat: 4g

Ingredients:

- 1 large eggplant, cut into ½" slices
- ½ cup whole wheat bread crumbs
- 3 tablespoons finely grated parmesan cheese
- Salt, to taste
- 1 teaspoon Italian seasoning mix
- 3 tablespoon whole wheat flour
- 1 free-range egg + 1 tablespoon water
- Olive oil spray
- 1 cup marinara sauce
- ¼ cup grated mozzarella cheese
- Fresh parsley or basil to garnish

Method:

1. Preheat your air fryer to 360°F.
2. Take a small bowl and combine the flour, egg and water. Stir well.
3. Take a shallow dish and add the breadcrumbs, parmesan, Italian seasoning and salt. Stir well to combine.
4. Dip the eggplant into the egg mixture, allow any excess to drip off then dip into the breadcrumbs.
5. Transfer into the air fryer and cook for 8-10 minutes until perfectly cooked.

Roasted Brussels Sprouts with Garlic and Thyme

More Brussels sprouts, but this time gently flavored with fragrant garlic and fresh herbs. Make sure you season the sprouts generously and you'll create a treat which transforms the whole idea of brussels sprouts and turn them into something utterly lovely.

Serves: 4
Time: 20 mins

- Calories: 79
- Net carbs: 8g
- Protein: 4g
- Fat: 2g

Ingredients:

- 1 lb. Brussels sprouts, cleaned and trimmed
- ½ teaspoon dried thyme
- 1 teaspoon dried parsley
- 4 cloves garlic, crushed
- ¼ teaspoon salt
- 2 teaspoons oil (opt.)

Method:

1. Preheat your air fryer to 390°F.
2. Grab a medium bowl and add all the ingredients. Stir well to combine.
3. Place into the air fryer and cook for 8-10 minutes until perfect.
4. Serve and enjoy.

Special Cauliflower Rice

Cauliflower rice is a great low carb alternative to regular rice which packs in a ton of extra nutrients. Used as a base for delicious Asian-inspired tofu and served with a ton of veggies, your taste buds will be in heaven.

Serves: 3
Time: 30 mins
- Calories: 153
- Net carbs: 18g
- Protein: 10g
- Fat: 4g

Ingredients:
For the tofu...
- ½ block firm or extra firm tofu, crumbled
- 2 tablespoons soy sauce
- ½ cup diced onion
- 2 carrots, diced
- 1 teaspoon turmeric

For the rice...
- 3 cups riced cauliflower
- 2 tablespoons reduced sodium soy sauce
- 1 ½ teaspoons toasted sesame oil, opt.
- 1 tablespoon rice vinegar
- 1 tablespoon minced ginger
- ½ cup finely chopped broccoli
- 2 cloves garlic, minced
- ½ cup frozen peas

Method
1. Preheat the air fryer to 370°F.
2. Grab a large bowl and add the tofu to the rest of the tofu ingredients. Stir well to combine.
3. Transfer to the air fryer and cook for 10 minutes.
4. Take another bowl and add the remaining ingredients. Stir well.
5. Place into the air fryer and cook for another 10 minutes.
6. Serve and enjoy.

Baked Sweet Potato Cauliflower Patties

If you have hungry kids coming home from school or you just want to create a healthy awesome snack, give these patties a try. They're an awesome low-carb way to stay fueled through the day and you can pimp them up with whatever veggies you have lying in the back of your fridge.

Serves: 1
Time: 35 mins
- Calories: 85
- Net carbs: 6g
- Protein: 2.7g
- Fat: 2.9g

Ingredients:
- 1 medium to large sweet potato, peeled and chopped
- 2 cups cauliflower florets
- 1 green onion, chopped.
- 1 teaspoon minced garlic
- 2 tablespoon ranch seasoning mix or paleo ranch seasoning
- 1 cup packed cilantro
- ½ teaspoon chili powder
- ¼ teaspoon cumin
- 2 tablespoons arrowroot powder
- ¼ cup ground flaxseed
- ¼ cup sunflower seeds
- Salt and pepper, to taste

To serve...
- Dipping sauce of choice

Method:
1. Preheat oven to 400°F.
2. Grab your food processor and add the sweet potato, cauliflower, onion and garlic. Whizz until smooth.
3. Open up and add the remaining ingredients. Hit that whizz button again until it forms a batter.
4. Using your hands, shape into patties and place onto a greased baking sheet.
5. Pop into the freezer for 10 minutes.
6. Open the freezer and transfer the patties to the air fryer.
7. Cook for 20 minutes, flipping halfway.

Tortilla Snack Chips

Put down the chips and make yourself these instead! All you need is a pack (or more!) or tortilla chips, a tiny amount of oil and your air fryer and you can create crunchy, moreish snacks which actually do you good. Get creative with spices and seasonings and you'll create something even more special!

Serves: 1-2
Time: 15 mins
- Calories: 50
- Net carbs: 10g
- Protein: 1g
- Fat: 1g

Ingredients:
- 1 x 8 pack tortillas of choice
- Cooking spray
- Salt to taste

Method:
1. Preheat your air fryer to 350°F.
2. Take a cookie cutter to slice the tortillas into rounds.
3. Spray the tortillas with cooking spray and sprinkle with salt.
4. Cook for 2-3 minutes.
5. Serve and enjoy.

Cheese Sticks

Cheese stick coating in crunchy, cheesy coatings?? Oooh don't mind if I do!

Makes: 8
Time: 17 mins
- Calories: 62
- Net carbs: 2g
- Protein: 4g
- Fat: 4g

Ingredients:
- 8 regular cheese sticks
- 1 large free-range egg
- ¼ cup almond flour
- ½ cup grated parmesan cheese
- 1 teaspoon Italian seasoning
- ¼ teaspoon ground rosemary
- 1 teaspoon garlic powder

Method:
1. Take shallow bowl and crack the egg inside. Whisk well.
2. Take another shallow bowl and add the almond flour, parmesan, Italian seasoning, rosemary and garlic powder. Stir well to combine.
3. Dip the cheese sticks into the egg, allow any excess to drip off then dip into the almond flour.
4. Place onto a lined baking sheet and pop into the freezer for 10 minutes.
5. Preheat the air fryer to 370°F.
6. Remove the cheese sticks from the freezer then pop into the air fryer.
7. Cook for 10 minutes, then serve and enjoy.

Sweets and Treats

Easy Coconut Pie

Even if you're the kind of person who destroys your cake before it even makes it into the oven, I promise that you can definitely make this coconut pie! Simply mix and throw into your air fryer and you're good to go.

Serves: 6-8

Time: 20 mins

- Calories: 507
- Net carbs: 17g
- Protein: 5g
- Fat: 50g

Ingredients:

- 2 free-range eggs
- 1 ½ cups milk
- ¼ cup butter
- 1 ½ teaspoon vanilla extract
- 1 cup shredded coconut
- ½ cup Monk Fruit sweetener
- ½ cup coconut flour

Method:

1. Preheat the air fryer to 350°F and grease a 6" pie plate. Pop to one side.
2. Grab a large bowl and add all the ingredients. Stir well to combine.
3. Pour onto the pie plate and pop into your air fryer.
4. Cook for 10-12 minutes until cooked through.
5. Serve and enjoy!

Cinnamon Donuts

Oh my goodness! These are soooo good! You'll never want to eat a regular donut when you've nibbled on these babies. They're ready fast, they're very low carb and they're super simple to make. Love them!

Serves: 10
Time: 15 mins

- Calories: 141
- Net carbs: 2g
- Protein: 4g
- Fat: 12g

Ingredients:

For the donuts...

- ½ cup sour cream
- ¼ cup heavy whipping cream
- 4 large free-range eggs
- 1 teaspoon vanilla extract
- ½ cup coconut flour
- ¼ teaspoon nutmeg
- ¼ teaspoon baking soda
- ¼ cup Erythritol
- Pinch of salt

For the cinnamon coating...

- ¼ cup Erythritol
- 1 teaspoon cinnamon
- ¼ cup coconut oil.

Method:

1. Preheat your air fryer to 360°F and grease a donut pan (that will fit into your air fryer).
2. Take a large bowl and add the sour cream, whipping cream, eggs and vanilla. Stir well to combine.
3. Add the dry ingredients to the bowl; the coconut flour, nutmeg, baking soda, erythritol and salt. Stir well to combine everything.
4. Pour the batter into the donut tin.
5. Place into the air fryer and cook for 15 minutes until perfect.
6. Serve and enjoy.

Gluten-Free Chocolate Lava Cake

Don't you just LOVE easy chocolate cakes like these ones?? Simply throw the ingredients into a bowl, stir and throw into your air fryer for a gooey, melted chocolate cake treat that will be yours, all yours! Feel free to increase the quantity if you're catering for more people.

Serves: 1
Time: 15 mins

- Calories: 269
- Net carbs: 13g
- Protein: 10g
- Fat: 23g

Ingredients:

- 1 free-range egg
- 2 tablespoons cocoa powder
- 2 tablespoons water
- 2 tablespoons erythritol
- 1/8 teaspoon Stevia
- 1 tablespoon golden flax meal
- 1 tablespoon coconut oil, melted
- ½ teaspoon aluminum-free baking powder
- Dash of vanilla extract
- Pinch of Himalayan salt

Method:

1. Preheat your air fryer to 350°F.
2. Take a large bowl and add all the ingredients. Stir well to combine.
3. Take a 2-cup glass ramekin and pour the batter inside.
4. Place into the air fryer and cook for 10 minutes.
5. Serve and enjoy.

Fried Cheesecake Bites

These mini cheesecake bites are a great party snack of wonderful for whenever you've had a hard day and need to give yourself a treat. Just five ingredients is all you need to make low carb, guilt-free treats that will leave you feeling utterly spoiled.

Makes: 16
Time: 45 mins
- Calories: 80
- Net carbs: 2g
- Protein: 2g
- Fat: 7g

Ingredients:
- 8 oz. cream cheese, at room temp
- ½ cup + 2 tablespoons erythritol
- 4 tablespoons cream, divided
- ½ teaspoon vanilla extract
- ½ cup almond flour

Method:
1. Grab a large bowl and add the cream cheese, ½ cup erythritol, vanilla and 2 tablespoons of the heavy cream.
2. Beat with a wooden spoon until smooth.
3. Line a baking sheet with paper and scoop out the batter, placing it on the sheet.
4. Pop into the freezer for 30 minutes.
5. Preheat your air fryer to 350°F.
6. Meanwhile, take a bowl and combine the almond flour with the rest of the erythritol and stir together.
7. Take another bowl and add the remaining cream.
8. Remove the bites from the freezer and dip into the cream, then roll in the almond flour.
9. Place into the air fryer and cook for 2-3 minutes.
10. Serve and enjoy.

Chocolate Almond Cupcakes

Not only are these chocolate almond cupcakes incredibly easy, they also melt in your mouth. Flecked with tiny chocolate chips and sweetened with maple syrup, they're real food that matters.

Serves: 5
Time: 25-30 mins
- Calories: 187
- Net carbs: 14g
- Protein: 3g
- Fat: 14g

Ingredients:
- 3 tablespoons butter
- 2 tablespoon real maple syrup
- ½ cup almond flour
- 1/8 teaspoon salt
- 1/3 cup chocolate chips
- 1 free-range egg, beaten
- ½ teaspoon vanilla

Method:
1. Preheat the air fryer to 320°F then prepare your silicone cake liners.
2. Grab a large bowl and combine the chocolate chips, butter, and honey.
3. Place a pan of water over a medium heat and bring to the boil then place the bowl on top.
4. Stir well until the chocolate melts.
5. Remove from the heat then add the remaining ingredients and stir well again.
6. Scoop the batter into the silicone cake cases then place into the air fryer.
7. Cook for 15-20 minutes then remove.
8. Allow to cool the dust with icing sugar (optional).
9. Serve and enjoy!

Brazilian Grilled Pineapple

You can keep your carbs under control whilst also spoiling your taste buds by indulging in this delicious, juicy pineapple. A taste of the tropical, it makes a wonderful summer desert when you want to feel spoiled!

Serves: 4
Time: 20 mins

- Calories: 295
- Net carbs: 24g
- Protein: 1g
- Fat: 8g

Ingredients:

- 1 small pineapple peeled, cored and cut into spears
- ½ cup sweetener
- 2 teaspoons ground cinnamon
- 3 tablespoons melted butter

Method:

1. Preheat your air fryer to 400°F.
2. Take a small bowl and add the sugar and cinnamon. Stir well to combine.
3. Place the pineapple onto a flat surface and brush with melted butter.
4. Sprinkle the sugar over the pineapple then place into the air fryer.
5. Cook for 6-10 minutes.
6. Serve and enjoy.

Spiced Apples

These apples make a wonderful healthy snack for kids or adults and a great healthy topping for your low carb oatmeal, your ice cream, or even as a low carb apple 'pie'. They're so good, I bet you'll finish the whole batch at once!!

Serves: 4
Time: 15 mins
- Calories: 160
- Net carbs: 30g
- Protein: 0g
- Fat: 7g

Ingredients:
- 4 small apples, sliced
- 2 tablespoons coconut oil, melted
- 2 tablespoons sweetener
- 1 teaspoon apple pie spice

Method:
1. Preheat the air fryer to 350°F.
2. Take a medium bowl and place the apples inside.
3. Cover with the melted coconut oil and stir well to coat.
4. Sprinkle with sugar and spice and toss to coat.
5. Pierce the apple with a fork then place into your air fryer for 10 minutes.
6. Serve and enjoy.

Flourless Chocolate Brownies

Chocolate brownies are one of my favorite deserts and they're also very easy to make in your air fryer. You only need five ingredients to make a wonderfully tender, gluten-free, low carb treat that will keep everyone's taste buds very happy. Enjoy!

Serves: 6
Time: 45 mins

- Calories: 224
- Net carbs: 23g
- Protein: 5g
- Fat: 24g

Ingredients:

- ½ cup sugar-free chocolate chips
- ½ cup butter
- 3 free-range eggs
- ¼ cup sweetener
- 1 teaspoon vanilla extract

Method:

1. Preheat your air fryer to 350°F and grease a springform tin that will fit into your air fryer.
2. Grab a microwave safe bowl and add the butter and chocolate. Pop into the microwave and warm for a minute until melted. Stir well and pop to one side.
3. Take a medium bowl and add the eggs, sweetener and vanilla. Whisk until frothy.
4. Add the melted chocolate and butter and stir well to combine.
5. Pour the batter in the tin and cook for 30 minutes.
6. Serve and enjoy.

Sweet Potato Dessert Fries

Fries don't need to be savory, as these jaw-droppingly good sweet fries prove. Dusted with cinnamon sugar and surprisingly satisfying to the bite, they'll add a ton of antioxidants to your diet whilst also satisfying your sweet tooth.

Serves: 2
Time: 25 mins
- Calories: 427
- Net carbs: 23g
- Protein: 1g
- Fat: 2g

Ingredients:
- 2 medium sweet potatoes, sliced lengthwise into ½" pieces
- ½ tablespoon coconut oil, melted
- 1 tablespoon arrowroot starch
- 2 teaspoon melted butter
- ¼ cup coconut sugar
- 1-2 tablespoons cinnamon

Method:
1. Preheat your air fryer to 370°F.
2. Place the sweet potatoes into a medium bowl with the melted coconut oil and arrowroot.
3. Stir well to combine then place into the air fryer for 18 minutes, shaking halfway through cooking.
4. Remove from the air fryer and place into a bowl.
5. Add the melted butter, sugar and cinnamon to the bowl and stir well to coat
6. Serve and enjoy!

Final Words

Feeling inspired? Ready to crack open your air fryer and get cooking some easy, nourishing, and delicious food? Of course you are!

Like many successful people, you have a busy life so you don't have time to waste on small talk or unnecessary details.

That's why I won't hang around here talking when you could be getting creative in the kitchen with your air fryer so let's round things up...

Throughout this book you've learned that the air fryer is the best piece of kitchen equipment that you can use to create crunchy, mouth-watering, indulgent, low carb foods with less mess, less fuss and, importantly, much less time.

Follow the low carb guidelines we've shared in the introduction and your dishes won't just be easy, they'll also be packed with nutrition and also be free from those unhealthy carcinogenic fats *and* they'll help you to look and feel at your best.

So now it's up to you to get cooking! Choose a handful of the most delicious-sounding recipes in this book, head to the grocery store and get cooking! That's the only way you can expand your cooking repertoire, improve your skills with your air fryer, learn how to cook mouth-watering and healthy low carb foods and save a ton of time.

Happy cooking!

Could you help?
I just wanted to say a quick thank you for downloading this cookbook- a lot of love has gone into writing these pages. I hope you've got a ton of value from learning some of the healthy low carb recipes that you can cook quickly and easily with your air fryer. It's been fun. *How has it been for you? ;)*

If you like what you've read, I'd really appreciate it if you could take a few seconds to **leave a review on Amazon**. It would make a big difference for me and my publishing career! Thank you!